The APE *in Our House*

The APE
in Our House

by Cathy Hayes

HARPER & BROTHERS — PUBLISHERS

New York

THE APE IN OUR HOUSE

FIRST EDITION

H-A

CONTENTS

760057

SIXTEEN PAGES OF PHOTOGRAPHS IN FOUR SECTIONS WILL BE FOUND FOLLOWING PAGES 72, 104, 136 and 200.

The APE *in* Our House

By Way of Introduction—

SCIENTIFIC curiosity, often operating under more pretentious names, has inspired some of mankind's greatest adventures. It has driven men with questions on their minds to the secret places of the earth, to the bottom of the sea, and out into the stratosphere. For some it has earned reputations as selfless servants of humanity while others, motivated by the same curiosity, are branded as rash meddlers in the affairs of nature. The persistent search for knowledge may result in poverty and long hours of labor in depressing circumstances. But sometimes curiosity turns life into a three-ring circus. And thus it was with us.

In the beginning my husband Keith and I were curious about chimpanzees. We wondered, for instance, why apes do not speak, and whether they could be taught to do so by special methods and great effort. Besides language, what distinguishes their behavior from that of people, we wondered? Can they adjust to the human way of life, and make use of the tools of our culture? Do they possess any real imitative

1

ability to back up the traditional phrase "monkey see, monkey do"? To get down to the basic problem: How intelligent are apes, in comparison with man?

These provocative questions and many more needled our curiosity until we determined to look for some of the answers by studying chimpanzees. But one cannot compare the inborn intelligence of man and ape by using civilized man and jungle ape. From the moment of birth distinctive educations begin widening the gap between the two species, rapidly obscuring their *innate* capacities with two different sets of experience.

Likewise, apes who have been raised in laboratory cages, while tremendously valuable in a great variety of studies, would be useless to us. Not only does the caged ape possess a personality distorted by imprisonment, but his opportunity to learn is restricted like his jungle cousin's. Our human tests would not apply to either.

The more we thought about it, the more obvious the answer became. If we were to use those evaluations of intelligence which had been designed for people, my husband and I must raise an ape from birth in the manner that humans are typically raised. We would then be able to rule out environmental influences and give a clear-cut description of the chimpanzee's inherited mental capacity. Gradually we formulated plans for our experiment. If we ever found the opportunity we would adopt a newborn baby chimpanzee and raise it as a human in all respects, giving it everything the human child needs: loving care, security, playmates, toys, and sympathetic guidance. We decided that such a chimpanzee must be observed constantly for its entire life span, which might well equal ours. During its course of development, its body and brain must be compared not only with human beings its own age, but also with caged apes. This home-raised chimpanzee would provide psychologists with an evaluation of basic anthropoid intelligence, and in addition, its unique upbringing would prepare our subject for a great many studies never before possible.

But all this was mere daydreaming, prompted by our restless curiosity. The idea of raising an ape like a child made interesting chatter around a Western campfire. Teaching an ape to say "mama" was a proposition which could liven up any party at the yawning stage, but like most fond dreams, it seemed to have little hope of fulfillment. Where did one acquire a newborn chimpanzee? How did one earn a living at this sort of thing?

Keith had just received his Ph.D. at Stanford University when our big chance came. He was offered his first job as a research psychologist by the Yerkes Laboratories of Primate Biology in Orange Park, Florida. Here was the perfect opportunity to do our experiment, for this is the world's largest research station for the study and breeding of chimpanzees. We were told that a baby chimp would be born toward the end of August. Keith accepted the job at once, we piled our belongings in the jalopy, and left our California home to keep a date across the continent with the yet unborn chimpanzee— Viki Hayes.

As in any scientific experiment, or in the rearing of any youngster, it is impossible to thank properly all those who have contributed to the project. Certainly everyone mentioned in the pages which follow has helped to shape Viki's unique personality. We were especially lucky to have the friendly encouragement, co-operation, and advice of three renowned scientists—Dr. Robert M. Yerkes, who founded the Laboratory; Dr. Karl S. Lashley, its present director; and Dr. Henry W. Nissen, assistant director. Dr. Nissen's share in our work began as early as 1929, when he returned from a field study of chimpanzees in Western French Guinea, bringing Viki's

father with him. He was able to give us much practical help,
for he has made a lifelong study of chimpanzees and is
credited with understanding all their dark and mysterious
facets. It is said that his rapport with these animals is second
only to Tarzan's.

And for giving a home and a welcome to strangers in a
strange land, our wonderful landlady Carrie Clarke rates as
an indispensable colleague.

Financially our research has been supported by generous
grants from the Penrose fund of the American Philosophical
Society, an honorary scientific organization dedicated to the
pursuit of knowledge. These have provided supplies for making
silent and sound movies, as well as equipment and some
outside help.

With the assistance of all her good friends, Viki has reached
a handsome, healthy age of three. This story will tell of our
life together in those three years, and of the beginnings of our
experiment, which is expected to run indefinitely. As I begin
our book, Viki is sitting on the back of my chair, brushing my
hair, so that we seem to represent the Hayes house totem
pole. Now she tugs at my sleeve, calling, "Mama! Mama!"
I will continue after I have given her the attention she requires—food, drink, or a session on the potty.

PART 1.

The First Eighteen Months

CHAPTER 1.

We Adopt a Baby

ON THE first September morning of 1947, we turned our car onto the main thoroughfare of Orange Park, Florida. A narrow boulevard, shaded by great live oaks and silvery Spanish moss, it ran through the little Southern town, past the usual assortment of fine ancestral homes and humble shanties, past country-style general stores, and a whistlestop station. There was little to distinguish Orange Park from scores of other small towns. Yet we drove slowly that morning and looked intently, for here we would make our home while my husband Keith worked as a research psychologist at the Yerkes Laboratories of Primate Biology. Here we would do our long-anticipated experiment, raising a baby ape in our house, in order to study chimpanzee intelligence.

Outside the village, the road dipped through a marshy stretch of turpentine woods. When it rose again, there stood the Laboratory: handsome white buildings set among semi-tropical vegetation, the whole enclosed by a stout electric fence. Out of sight of the road, but within easy hearing, was our journey's end, cage after cage of climbing, pounding, noisy chimpanzees.

Director Karl S. Lashley escorted us around the establishment, describing the work in progress, introducing us to the staff, man and animal. He pointed out by name chimpanzees of every age and personality, and showed us the kitchen where their food is prepared, the offices and research rooms, the library, and the shop where apparatus is built.

To us, the most interesting department was the nursery where the baby apes are taken soon after birth. If left with their mothers, not only would the babies suffer from uncontrolled and often erratic care and feeding, but they could not be used in the many important studies of infant chimpanzees being done at the Laboratory. Presiding over the nursery was Annie Jones, who was preparing lunch for her six charges when we arrived. She was slicing apples and oranges into a pan which already held small ripe bananas. The rest of the table was covered with bottles of milk and tomato juice, some with nipples over the tops, some with cups.

The two oldest babies, rowdy two-year-olds, were banging the bars of an outdoor sunporch. In an indoor cage, four-month-old Beti clutched her diaper and rocked nervously from side to side when she saw us. Two smaller babies slept in little white cribs, sucking their thumbs. They were all cute chimpanzee children, but when I tried to play with them, they screamed and clung to Annie for protection.

In addition to its own kitchen and the infant's living quarters, the nursery includes a large utility room, where Annie dries the diapers which the babies use in great numbers, and where experimenters work with the youngsters. As Dr. Lashley moved among the apparatus, explaining its use, he came to a small cardboard box. Bending over it, he beckoned to us, saying, "I guess this is the one you'll have."

I felt my knees go shaky, for his remark had taken me unawares. Fascinated by the older animals, I had momentarily forgotten why we were here. Now from the box came a baby-soft "Oo oo, oo oo," and a tiny brown hand began clawing the air above it. I held out a finger, the little hand found it and hung on tightly. While we stared appalled at the small size and huge ugliness of the creature in the box, it stopped crying. It seemed to examine us, too, but of course the infant's eyes did not yet focus on anything, for she had arrived at the Laboratory only three days ahead of us.

Like any newborn baby, a three-day-old chimpanzee is beautiful only to its mother. This one looked like a monstrous spider, with long skinny arms and legs thrashing out from a solid potbelly. Most of her scant four pounds was concentrated in that middle, which was topped by an adhesive tape navel dressing. The skin of her body was light brown, taut and shiny-smooth. In contrast her face was crinkled into deep, moist grooves, so that her head looked like nothing so much as a head-hunter's trophy. Stiff black hair stood out from her head and cheeks, conspiring with wide vacant eyes to give an expression of terror and resentment. And always her right hand swept up in an arc, sifting the air like a barnacle at feeding time, searching for a mama to cling to. This was Viki in the beginning.

They had named her Viki—a name which is said to combine the names of her parents, Vera and Bokar. Like so many little girls who rise to higher things, Viki was born to simple, honest folks, unpretentious, but good, solid stock. Vera and Bokar are jungle-born apes who have earned reputations at the Yerkes Laboratory for being even-tempered, healthy, and of average intelligence. Only in the matter of beauty are they considered exceptional and their daughter showed little promise in that category.

We took over her care immediately, although she would

remain in the nursery until we could find suitable housing. I spent most of every day beside her crib, observing her behavior and tending her needs. I was instantly amazed at the strength in her tiny grasp, which almost turned our first contact into a tragedy. I picked her up too suddenly, and in her panic-stricken search for something to hang onto, she found her own ear. Only the promptest action on my part preserved her jug-eared symmetry. Her prehensile chimpanzee feet were every bit as strong and clingy as her hands. As she slept she clutched the bedding, and when I pried her loose for feeding or diaper changes, she transferred her grasp to my clothing. To put her down I had to undo her clutching, hand by hand, foot by foot, and then hand by hand again. I never had a moment's worry about dropping her. Their infants' ability to hang on must be a great comfort to ape mothers in the jungle, and is no doubt partly responsible for survival in arboreal life.

Before she was a month old Viki could cross her crib in odd "swimming" movements, made by pulling herself across the bed pad while she pushed with her knobby knees. Clasping my thumb, she could suspend her own weight by one arm for more than a minute. She held her head erect, and in her eagerness for food, she began to raise her whole body free of the bed pad and wait trembling on hands and knees as I approached with the bottle. By this time her eyes followed me as well as the bottle though considerably more interested in the latter. So voracious was her appetite that sometimes while eating she clutched my hand which held the bottle and pushed her feet against my lap until she was actually standing up to eat—this at four weeks of age!

If Viki's early strength was surprisingly different from the newborn child's weakness, even more so was the fact that she never cried. We considered ourselves fortunate at the time, but later we came to look with awe upon the crying of the human infant as the first step toward speech. Viki had an apprehensive little "oo oo, oo oo" which burst into a scream under stress, but she did not whimper or give any vocal indication that she needed food, a burping, or dry diapers. Being a quiet baby is probably also essential for jungle survival.

Almost at once Viki began adjusting to the vagaries of civilization. Her first real accomplishment was learning that when the nipple of her bottle collapsed, she must not keep dragging on it, but release it a moment until it filled with air. I did not teach her the physical principle involved, nor did I know what was happening until Keith explained it. Here at one month the pattern of our family was formed. Viki did it. I observed it. Keith explained it.

Unfortunately Keith is better at explaining things than he was at finding a landlord who would accept a chimpanzee tenant. We had temporary rooms, but the owners wanted no part of Viki. We were anxious to begin our work, and in addition were having trouble getting acclimated to the incessant humid heat of the tropical storm season. A phenomenal insect population and whirling eddies of sand added to our miseries.

For days we huddled on the edge of a hurricane. It was nerve-racking until the storm struck as close as it would. The rain came in sheets that brightened the trailing Spanish moss to green against the red pine bark. Palm fronds waved like big hands. The air was loud with the rushing, cracking, howling sounds of a tropical storm. Above the wind the big apes screamed in terror. Up in a nursery window I sat with Viki in my arms, watching the storm wear itself out.

When the rains were over, the sand appeared again. Once more the ants, the fleas, and roaches descended upon us. And we despaired of ever finding Viki a home. Then two of our new

colleagues, Josephine and Bob Blum, who lived a mile down
the road at the Pecan Grove, learned that the lower flat of
their duplex was being vacated. They hurried to their landlady, Carrie Clarke, with a good word for us, tactfully neglect-
ing to mention our baby.

Hardly daring to hope, we dressed our little ape in her
first knitted T-shirt, the tiniest size available but still volumi-
nous on her. We placed her on a soft blue blanket in her
covered picnic basket, and headed for Clarke's Pecan Grove.
It was cool in the shadows of the great pecan trees. The
houses were large and airy-looking and flowers bloomed everywhere. Leaving Viki in the car, we sought out Mrs. Clarke.
We liked her instantly. She was no more than five feet tall,
with friendly eyes and a laughing mouth, and she welcomed
us warmly. While I tried to tell her that there was more to our
family than met the eye, Keith went to the car for Viki. With
a fine air of resignation, he placed the picnic basket at Mrs.
Clarke's feet.

"What do you have here?" she asked as she lifted the lid.
We held our breath. Then her characteristically roguish grin
softened into a smile. "Well, will you look at that," she murmured gently, and we knew we were in.

The apartment was small but adequate, a living-dining
room, a large bedroom to share with Viki, kitchen and bath.
There was a spacious yard which Viki would need later on.
Our only close neighbors were the Blums upstairs, who worked
at the Laboratory all day, adored chimpanzees, and would not
mind living with one. Best of all, Mrs. Clarke from that day to
this has fondly referred to Viki as "our baby."

While I prepared for her homecoming, Keith cared for
Viki at the Laboratory and built her special furniture. To the
standard tiny crib she had been using was added a mattress
and bedding. He built a low table, fifty-four inches square

with a seat depressed into one end, where Viki would sit to take her meals, or rather to work for them. A small green potty was constructed to be set over our toilet, for Viki was to be toilet-trained. Into our bathtub Keith fitted a removable shelf, the "diaper board," on which Viki would have her diapers changed.

Now we were ready to begin our experiment, and one moonlit night while a mockingbird sang in some far-off corner of the Pecan Grove, we brought Viki home.

CHAPTER 2.

Vegetative Phase

THE six-week-old Viki responded to her new home and loving caretakers with all the enthusiasm of the vegetables which I bring home from my weekly trips to market. As a matter of fact, she was mighty like a vegetable. For endless hours she nestled in her cozy bed. Now and then she absorbed some liquid nourishment, and shortly afterward gave off a bit of water or other waste products. She shifted her position occasionally, or took a firmer grip on her environment as any good potato does. But mostly she just waited, and grew larger, and slept and slept and slept.

We had no way of knowing how much she could observe or learn at this time, but not wanting to lose our advantage in getting her young, we immediately began beaming civilization at her. As part of her education, a small radio next to her bed played softly but incessantly. Some of our new colleagues said that this shouldn't happen to an ape. Others contended that this was just about radio's level of aspiration.

Whenever I noticed her lying awake, I picked her up for some concentrated mothering. Each day she was given an

14

exercise period on our bed while I tried to interest her in her first toys, selected for color, size, or fascinating noise. As I talked to her, however, she only stared at me, and her wrinkled little deadpan never assumed the slightest expression.

Her first formal lessons, at six weeks of age, were in toilet training, by coincidence the one area of her education in which we have been most eminently unsuccessful. After feeding her, we rushed her to the bathroom. The results do not seem nearly so remarkable in retrospect, considering that we, and not Viki, were becoming educated—to make the mad dash. Nevertheless, we proudly announced that Viki, still too young to sit unsupported on the potty, was completely toilet-trained. The people at the Laboratory congratulated us with quiet smiles. (When in another six weeks Viki's first steps disrupted the "habit," they smiled just as quietly and said, "Well, you have to expect that." For the remainder of her first three years, Viki has vacillated between complete toilet training and utter lack of control almost as frequently as I turn the pages of the calendar.)

Viki began to work for food on her first day at home. The problem was very simple. As I snuggled her close to me, I held the bottle in my hand with my thumb sticking out like a handle. With the efficiency and dispatch she quickly applied to all problems involving food, Viki learned to grasp my thumb and pull the bottle toward her. This was no idle game, for if Viki was to become educated, she must develop the ability to perceive a problem and solve it.

In the short stretches between feedings, Viki slept in her crib, or lay on the couch, mouthing toys. She could neither sit nor stand unaided, nor even turn over by herself. Bright or swiftly moving objects caught her glance, but she seldom handled toys. Our closest contact was when I bathed her. As a child I had rejected dolls, but now some latent mother instinct drove me to brushing and oiling my little ape in a frantic attempt to make her beautiful. But no amount of grooming could erase her wild startled expression, the deep moist wrinkles under her eyes, or the spindly appearance of her arms and legs. When I had made the most of the material at hand, I dressed her and tucked her into bed. There she usually sputtered a few rudimentary cusswords, gave me a belligerent glare, and fell asleep again.

While Viki slept I washed diapers, sterilized bottles, made formula, and in my spare time got acquainted with Florida, which is at its best in October and November. After a humid, bug-bitten summer and the September storms, the world seems fresh and livable. The unbelievably blue sky is streaked with wind-blown clouds and the air is cool and dry.

One afternoon as I dozed in the warm sun, anticipating a winter in Florida, I heard a rustle in the grass behind my chair. I turned, expecting to see one of the blue-tailed lizards that run in and out under our house. Instead I saw a slender snake about two feet long and more exquisite than any creature I have ever seen. Shiny golden lines circled its body between bands of jet black and red. For a long moment I stood hypnotized by its burnished Oriental-type beauty. Then with a cold fear I knew that I was looking at the most poisonous reptile in America, the deadly coral snake.

It was relatively motionless as it slowly swallowed a lizard, but I was not yet schooled in the practical art of doing in a snake. Making sure that Viki was safe in her bed (an irrational precaution considering that she had no means of locomotion), I ran for help. A two-wheeled mule cart was rattling down the road, and walking behind it was Robert Jacob, who tends the Grove for Mrs. Clarke. He was at the moment gathering pecans, but when he heard my news, he came running with a pitchfork. I begged him not to lacerate the skin and went into the house for a specimen jar.

When I returned, Robert was dangling the snake on the tines of his pitchfork, twisting it over and over, like an elusive strand of spaghetti. He had somehow gotten the idea that I wanted to keep it as a pet. When I explained that I wanted to preserve it, but in a thoroughly dead condition, he pressed a tine through the serpent's head without a moment's hesitation. The story caused some local excitement, and several people came to see the rare but much-feared snake.

I think it was these visitors to the snake who first saw Viki and told Orange Park about the strange ménage in the Pecan Grove. They met the infant Viki with mixed opinions written on their faces. We instructed everyone to act as if they were meeting a child and some threw themselves wholeheartedly into this make-believe. Others watched us feed and burp and diaper her, tongue in cheek, while still others felt the need to assert their broadmindedness. One man drove up to our house and blew his horn until I went out to see what he wanted. "Is this where the baby ape lives?" he asked. "Bring her out, will you? That I'd like to see." So far as I know, that man has yet to see his first home-raised ape.

A few visitors resented our taboos against handling, although this was actually Viki's own restriction. Our firmest rule was that no one with a cold should be permitted to come into the same room with Viki. We explained that apes seem to be particularly susceptible to respiratory troubles and that pneumonia is a major killer of chimpanzees. In those early days we worried constantly that Viki would catch a cold.

Viki ignored the visitors unless they greeted her with loud or sudden words. Then she uttered an explosive sputter which sounded like "uh uh uh uh." Since her vocal repertoire included little more than this, her worried "oo oo," and a shrill scream of fear, people expressed doubt that she would ever be able to talk.

The most frequent cause for her scream at this time was an urgent matter to a two-month-old chimpanzee. As her hands moved around in a random fashion, they often met, and because of her strong grasp reflex, they would grip each other fiercely. Unable to get free from her own clutches, Viki would scream until we pried her loose. After several weeks of constant crisis, Viki learned to let go. Then her fingers became intriguing toys as she watched them flex and intertwine, capture and escape from each other. She immediately made practical use of her new skill of being able to let go by very precisely grabbing and putting aside any hand that presumed to pick her nose.

In spite of our virtually requiring a health certificate from all callers, and our constant watch on temperature, humidity and drafts, when Viki was nine weeks old she caught a terrific cold. Since the Laboratory apes and people play host to the same cold germs, they pass colds back and forth quite freely. All winter long colds shuttle from office to cage to office to nursery and back again. I took Viki to the Laboratory one day to weigh her on the baby scales, and twenty-four hours after exchanging barks with the runny-nosed babies, Viki burst into loud rapid-fire sneezing. The cold soon established itself into long stretches of wheezing sleep broken by fits of sneezing and nasal discharge. We sent a hurried call for Henry Nissen, who administers to Viki's relatives in similar troubles. When he saw her at her worst, thirty-six hours after exposure, he threw a scare into us. He said that if she began to gasp in a certain way characteristic of pneumonia, we should rush her to the Laboratory for sulfa. I was awake all night listening for a change in her breathing, and shaking Keith to ask if he thought she was gasping *now*.

For three days she lay listlessly in her crib, looking miserable. When I picked her up, she whimpered a little as she drooped in my arms. We hung a cradle gym in her crib to amuse and exercise her during her confinement, but she ignored it. All that we could do was to keep her warm and nourished while we listened to her breathing. On the fourth day, as suddenly as it had begun, her sneezing stopped and her nose ceased its dripping. She became restless, and began to rock so fast and furiously that her whole crib shook from side to side. When I tried to separate her from her noon bottle, which she was gulping too fast, she gave a lusty scream and I knew that Viki was well.

She emerged from her first illness with a whoop and a yell. She tore the cradle gym from its moorings and dashed it to the floor. She ripped her bed sheet to pieces and tossed the shreds over the side. Thereafter her mattress was sewn into stout waterproof sheeting. She no longer needed blankets since Keith at this point installed in her crib a heater made of a tin can with a light bulb inside and a thermostat to keep her nest at a comfortable 75°. He also put a hinged top on the bed since he expected Baby to acquire a wanderlust in the near future. While this is scarcely a standard baby bed, it has saved Viki from the standard threats of pneumonia and strangulation.

Viki's first two teeth poked through at twelve weeks and we innocently rejoiced. In another two weeks two more teeth made their appearance, and she began gnawing on all available things and people. We offered her bananas as a substitute and here was her own idea of food.

The chore by which she earned her food was made a little harder. Instead of pulling my hand toward her she now had to pull a string which was tied around the bottle. When she had learned this, we held it farther away so that she had to grasp the string, pull, let go, take a second grip nearer the bottle, and pull once more. In a few weeks she learned the sailor's technique of pulling in hand over hand.

She learned to turn from back to front and back again, and entertained herself rolling over and over on our bed. One day on the couch she lifted her body to all fours and stood teetering uncertainly for a moment. Before she flopped down again, she had gone forward first one, and then two shuffling steps.

She began to pay some attention to her toys and her parents. She greeted us, and invariably sputtered her "uh uh uh uh," when she heard Keith's hearty and infectious laugh. She smiled a four-toothed grin when we tickled her, and one day as she panted in the sheer ecstasy of being tickled, a breathy staccato sound escaped from her throat. It was Viki's first laugh.

With a few learned methods for obtaining food, a few baby teeth, a few motor skills for moving about in the world, and the beginnings of social awareness, our Viki was no longer a vegetable.

CHAPTER 3.

Viki's First Christmas

"BUT honestly, Keith, it's like having one arm tied behind me. Or being pregnant all the time. Or both. I have no private life." I was complaining that Viki at four months was too much with me. From the moment she left her crib until she was tucked in at night, with time out for only an hour's nap, she clung to me like a papoose without benefit of knapsack. She sat on my lap while I ate or studied. She straddled my hip as I cooked. If she were on the floor, and I started to get away, she screamed and clung to my leg until I picked her up. I had expected this in a tiny infant, but now she was getting bigger and heavier and was able to get around by herself. I thought the time had come to start cutting the cord.

Keith agreed with me. "When it's inconvenient to carry her, put her down," he said. "She can walk by herself. Put her down and be firm about it."

But every time I tried to do so, Viki held up her furry little arms, pouted her lips, and cried, "Oo oo, oo oo."

"Oh, Keith, I don't want her to feel rejected," I said, softening. "She likes me, and I like her, and she's so little, and—"

21

"Cathy!" snapped the master. "Either be her slave and tote her around in silence, or put her down, but be firm about it. Be firm!"

At this point a distressed crescendo of "oo oo's" would drown out his words, and hoisting Viki to one hip, I would go to stir the soup while Keith shook his head sadly. My husband has all the qualities recommended for a parent. Calm and consistent, he has a fine sense of values and the relative importance of things, plus that elusive virtue of being "gentle but firm." From the beginning Viki obeyed him better, but identified herself more with me. I am very different from Keith, gay and depressed without warning, suspicious, possessive, quick to anger but just as quick to forgive—all common chimpanzee traits.

So Viki clung to me, or if I succeeded in putting her down, she tagged in my wake, "oo oo'ing" when I went too fast. If some rare lack of vigilance on her part let a room's length separate us, she came charging across the abyss, screaming at the height of her considerable ability. No woman could resist such evidence of need. Naturally I picked her up and toted her. While I made what may have been a misguided concession to her chimpanzee forebears, I rationalized that clinging for her was a matter of reflex, and that to frustrate it might disturb her psychologically.

In preparing for Viki's first Christmas, I discovered what a variety of chores can be performed one-handed. I built the cookies and fruit cake, wrapped presents, drew the chimpanzee Santa Clauses on our homemade cards, all with Viki firmly attached to me. As I carried her, supporting her bottom with my left hand, she clutched my upper arms so tightly that my biceps were always sore. I did not fully realize the power of a baby chimpanzee's grip until the day I read the account by Henry Nissen of a young ape whose grasp had given him bruises. I thought: Surely Henry exaggerates. Nevertheless I examined my upper arms in a mirror. To my surprise they were covered with black and blue spots the size of her finger tips. In addition there were old yellow bruises and a few red scabs where her nails had dug out bits of me.

Although she obviously preferred being carried, Viki could get around very well by her fourth month. She walked on all fours, on the knuckles of her hands and with her feet either flat or clenched. Her first steps were very amusing. She was so tiny yet so determined as she raised each bent bowleg in turn and set it down emphatically. Her arms gave her no trouble, but sometimes one leg would strike out behind her at an uncertain angle and paw the air as it searched for the floor. All the while her eyes would fixate dead ahead like a tight-rope walker who pulls himself to his destination by staring at it. Eventually her walking altered her whole personality, for it enlarged her environment and permitted her to satisfy her curiosity. It also encouraged social development. She began to examine callers, very tentatively at first, in brief sojourns away from mama.

One day Viki discovered that she could climb. She chinned herself on the edge of the couch, tossed over one leg, as a horse is mounted, and pushed up the rest of the way against the inner side of her knee. Then she ran into the problem every baby chimpanzee has to face, namely, how to get down. They usually learn to climb *up* long before they learn to descend. Annie tells me that during the first few days after Laboratory babies learn to climb, they spend many unhappy moments stranded at the wire-mesh ceilings of their cages until she rescues them. Viki would get up on the couch easily enough, and then stand crying at the edge while I tried to coax her down a makeshift stile of pillows and the footstool.

One by one I took away the pillows and Viki learned to bellyflop down those that remained, clutching the slipcover to break her fall. When the last pillow was gone, she gazed over the edge in terror, but since I was threatening to move away, she gathered up her courage and tumbled down any which way.

This now became one of her first "games," clasping her hands to her head and hurtling off the cliff. Then she laughed and climbed up to try it again—unless she saw us watching her. In that case she lay helplessly "oo oo'ing" on the floor, begging to be picked up.

Another characteristic she now developed in common with the Laboratory babies was a great fear of anything new that came into her life. If she suddenly spied Robert at work in the yard, she clung to me nervously until he went away. Toward the animals whom she would later chase out of the Grove, she now maintained a jittery silence. These included the mule who occasionally grazed at our back door, the neighborhood cows, hanging over our fence to eat the bushes, the pigs who invaded the yard, and a host of stray dogs and cats.

One day as I carried the electric heater from the bedroom to the bathroom, trailing the cord, Viki startled violently on my left arm and began screaming. Looking down I saw the heater cord snaking along behind us. Since she had outgrown her fear of the heater itself, I thought: Perhaps it is *true* that chimpanzees have an instinctive fear of snakes. After that whenever I carelessly dangled the heater cord, she went into paroxysms of fear, and I philosophized upon the ancient enmity of primate and serpent. But then one day as we played on the lawn, a black racer snake passed within three inches of us and slithered under the house. To my surprise Viki merely looked mystified. I later offered her a dead rat snake and she played with it happily. I trailed it along the ground and right over her feet, and she made no fuss at all. But the instant her eyes fell upon the heater cord, a frown appeared, her face flushed, and she burst out screaming. What was I to conclude except that Viki had an instinctive fear of electric-heater cords?

Most of her fears were just that irrational. Any new toy, a spot of light reflected on the ceiling, the taking off of her shoes—these were suddenly feared and just as abruptly accepted. One day she registered fear throughout her bath. The next day she was again eating soapsuds and laughing as the spray tickled her chest. Viki was even afraid of herself the first time she caught sight of her reflection in a small round shaving mirror. She flopped down and rocked in the manner of nervous chimpanzees. But she was too fascinated to remain frightened for long. She slowly rose to all fours and edged up to the mirror, staring steadily at her image all the time, until suddenly she lunged forward and looked behind it. Then she flopped down on her tummy again and rocked, very mystified. It reminded Keith of his childhood dog Ginger who once entered a room where a stuffed deer head hung on the wall. Ginger stood stock still, bristling and growling at the head. Then in a flash he raced into the next room, and stared transfixed at the spot where he should logically have seen the rest of the deer.

Viki became fond of the mirror, glancing coyly at it sideways, and making faces with her facile chimpanzee lips, but she was a year old before she stopped looking behind the mirror for the rest of the chimpanzee.

In spite of all her strange fears, so long as her world remained fairly constant, and her mama did not take off for parts unknown, Viki was essentially a happy little thing. Her most characteristic expression was one of intelligent inquiry with wide eyes and with a small smile playing around her lips.

She went into spells of stretching and nuzzling against the sofa cushions, smiling at us slyly between her legs as she worked her head into the pillows. If, moved by her small sweetness, we scooped her up in a hug, she usually burst into laughter.

Now that her gangling potbellied infancy was gone, Viki had become a beautiful animal. Her shiny coat of black hair stood out softly, giving her a stocky appearance. The skin underneath, pale brown at birth, was now chalk white, though her face, hands, and feet were still a pretty suntan color. With her flat nose, big ears, eyebrow ridges and retreating chin, she looked "like a chimpanzee ought to look." Her eyes, however, were exceptionally fine and expressive. The whites are in reality only slightly lighter than the reddish-brown irises, which gives an effect of greater size and brilliance.

I suddenly realized how pretty she had become on the eve of her first Christmas. I had suggested to Keith that he ask in a few people, and never a man for halfway measures, he invited everybody. First to arrive was Henry Nissen, who said to Viki, "You're getting prettier every day." She accepted this compliment with a stream of chatter. By her second Christmas she would be begging for cookies by saying "mama" but now her remarks consisted of such obscurities as "ee-oo" and "wha-ee."

While Viki entertained Henry, we lit the candles which would substitute for a tree, and assembled the makings of root-beer floats, the Hayes house version of eggnog at that time. The others arrived, the Blums, the Schillers, and finally, breathless on his bicycle, our Chinese colleague, Chow. Viki greeted each in turn with a loud chimp bark or a soft "goo-oh" depending on the heartiness of their hello. As the party got under way she sat at my feet with a firm grip on my ankles. Henry asked if this was not pretty hard on stockings. I sang the praises of nylons as the perfect hose for ape mothers. I offered the theory that she might be clinging to the stockings themselves rather than my legs since she seemed to cherish empty nylons just as much. Always the scientist, Henry tested this hypthesis by offering Viki his own leg, which boasted no nylons. Viki only took a firmer grip on my ankles and stared from the unquestionable beauty of his male leg up into his face and back at the leg again. All the psychologists then discussed the significance of this.

As everyone showed signs of remaining stationary—and our small room discouraged much traffic—Viki began making sly infiltrations into the crowd. She prowled from Chow's shoes to Mrs. Schiller's ·purse to her nylons and then beat a hasty retreat to my chair. When the people laughed at her eccentric gallop, she sputtered back at them and something approaching social contact was established. Bob Blum amused himself by threatening to catch her. This made her dash to my skirt helter-skelter. A crisis arose when we ladies went to the kitchen to replenish the root-beer floats. In the scramble Viki grabbed a hold on someone else's hem besides mine while she sputtered at Bob over her shoulder. When she happened to glance up and see her horrible mistake, she yipped, and climbed right up my dress front.

The only instances of social ease were with Henry and Chow. She played peekaboo with Henry, peeking breathlessly around the pillow they used as a barricade, and laughing as if she were being tickled when he "caught" her. Chow fed her cookies, meanwhile demonstrating the very peculiar elasticity of her chimpanzee lips. If he held a cookie to her lower lip, it came out to a point as he slowly withdrew the lure. If he now ran the cookie around her mouth, just out of reach of the protruded lip, the tiny point rippled around her lips, following the cookie in a continuous undulation.

As the candles burned low, and the supply of root beer gave out, Viki became what is called "cranky" in a child. She insisted on pulling my hair, and if I presumed to pay any attention to my duties as hostess, she cried "Bra! Bra!" in a shrill insistent way. Our guests wagered that if Viki ever did learn to speak spontaneously, her first words would be, "Please give me your undivided attention."

Viki spent Christmas Day mouthing her first doll, a plush monkey, and slapping at a small rubber dog which squeaked when pressed. Although she seemed to fear it, she was unable to resist sneaking up to it and whacking it with the back of her hand. In a few days she began lunging at it ferociously, throwing herself upon it and laughing, but she would not take it in her hands. Chimpanzees are very protective of their hands. Viki's rejection of an object is not to seize it and risk being seized, but to hit it away with the back of her hand, her wrist, or even her elbow.

We had a dinner party on Christmas night, but before we fed the people, we made them watch Viki at work on her new problem. As she sat in her work table, her bottle of food was mounted on a little cart to which was attached a long string. Simple as this sounds, considering that she had already learned to pull the string when I held the bottle, a week elapsed before she did it equally well on the table. When we then placed a second unbaited string alongside the first, she pulled whichever string her hand happened to touch first, often the wrong one, all the while staring at the bottle!

This is not to imply that Viki was stupid for her age. Rather it points out that even such a seemingly automatic response as the eyes and hands working together must be learned with great and lengthy difficulty. Every human being has to *learn* these same principles which were puzzling Viki.

Sometimes Viki resents being packed off to bed, and she

barks at us from inside her crib, but she offered no resistance after the excitement of the holiday. I left the top up until I had gathered her scattered playthings. As I straightened up with the last of these, I saw two brown hands creep over the top of her crib as Viki pulled herself to standing. A month before only the top of her head would have shown. A couple of weeks later two shiny brown eyes could peek over the edge. Now as I watched, her whole face came into view. Hanging her chin over the side, she smiled and said, "Goo-ah." And in her voice and her expression was the infinite happy fatigue shared by children everywhere on Christmas night.

CHAPTER 4.

Grandma Visits the Creature

AS A gray windy February turned slowly into spring, Grandma came visiting and Viki entertained her first house guest. Rather I should say she tolerated her visitor, for Viki at six months was apprehensive of all people and most things. We welcomed this early opportunity to expose her to a full-time stranger in the house. Since the rest of the family had accepted Viki as a bona fide Hayes, I eagerly anticipated the firsthand impressions of the traveling member of the clan. I had visions of a gentle granny crooning an old-fashioned lullaby to her precious great-grandchild.

Hah! Grandma's first words, with a quick glance about the room, were, "Where is that creature?" As for Viki, she barked and edged away with her hair standing on end.

When such pleasantries were over, we found ourselves at loose ends, so I busied myself by giving Viki a bath in her current tub, the shallow kitchen sink. Grandma stood in the doorway watching us, talking about all the places she had been since last we met, about her trip from Milwaukee and how she won $1.58 playing gin rummy with a salesman from

Kenosha. Now and then her voice wandered and then I noticed her keen old eyes sizing up the relationship between Viki and myself. Finally she stopped talking altogether, and watched entranced. Viki was trying to catch the stream of water in her hand, protruding her tummy against the warm spray, and sticking out her pink tongue to catch the drips from her arms.

Then came the drying process, the most endearing moments I spent with Viki at this time. While I patted and rubbed, Viki smiled broadly and nuzzled into the soft towel. Looking down at the fluffy ball of warm, fragrant baby, Grandma conceded, "I can see how you might come to love such a one, yes."

She reached out to stroke the baby's head. Viki bit her.

This amiable state of affairs continued for two days. Grandma so completely upset her home life that the little one followed me constantly, never taking her eyes off the intruder. When I held Viki's hands for practice sessions of upright walking, every muscle was tense. She did not play with her toys, or run, or climb on the furniture. Nor was Grandma her usual relaxed self. She held a certain aversion to our unorthodox baby, but still she could see that we loved Viki; to Grandma, "her children" can do no wrong. No doubt, also, her feelings were hurt by Viki's snarling display of fourteen baby teeth at her every approach.

Only on the potty did Viki behave normally, and she spent most of Grandma's visit on the potty. She had seemed to be toilet-trained, but the advent of a house guest had disrupted the habit once more. The sight of Viki on the potty threw Grandma into convulsions of laughter. The minute she saw me herding Viki toward the bathroom, she brought her knitting to the big chair opposite the open bathroom door, there to sit and watch the show. She chuckled merrily and applauded like

a child at a circus while Viki counted off the roll of toilet
paper, sheet after endless sheet. Reaching behind her, the
little ape brought down the stack of diapers in a shower. She
put her foot down into the hole. Hooking her arms under the
restraining bar, she tilted herself and the potty perilously backward. If Grandma laughed, Viki would stick out her chest and
assume her brazen "King Kong" look. Or she would unlatch
the bar and bang it defiantly. Or standing with her back to
Grandma, she would bend over and peek through her legs at
the visitor. Grandma kept saying, "Now I've seen everything."

We took Viki on her first trip while Grandma was here. Into
the back seat we packed the crib, the potty, diapers, a basket
of lunch, and Grandma, and drove to Marineland. This is
essentially a small piece of ocean isolated in a huge tank for
amusement and study.

For the journey Viki wore a dainty blue sweater with a
matching bonnet which came to a peak at the crown. Her
sideburns poked out around the edges, framing her funny little
face like a ruffle. She would have melted a sterner heart than
Grandma's. While Viki amused herself by playing with my
clothes and purse, Grandma tried to keep posted on "what she
was doing now." Occasionally Viki flung herself over my
shoulder to glare and sputter at Grandma, who sputtered back
a gay reply.

Her first hour of motoring lulled Viki to sleep and we
tucked her into her crib with the top down, a blanket thrown
over the front to cut out wayward drafts. A little while later I
was struck by the beauty of a young swamp maple sending
forth new red leaves through the gray moss. I turned to call it
to Grandma's attention and caught her peeking under the
blanket. She straightened up and tried to look unconcerned,
but she said, "The creature looks cute—when it's asleep."

South of St. Augustine we parked on a deserted sand dune

and ate our lunch. I fed Viki her tomato juice, and then we scooped a hole in the rippling pattern of the sand and set her potty over it. Resplendent in her hand-knit finery, Viki sat looking out over the Atlantic which her parents had crossed a brief quarter century before. I could not help having thoughts of nature and nurture, and of the immigrant's child in the Land of Opportunity.

Viki slept in the car while we visited Marineland and marveled at their porpoises. The amusing antics, the grace and control of these animals was a source of scientific wonder to us and sheer fascination to that perfect tourist who is our Grandma.

On the way home, Viki was very much awake again, munching on a banana and the oranges which Grandma peeled for us. Stopping for a red light in downtown St. Augustine, Keith spoke to Viki and she turned her face to him for an exchange of grins and chatter. On the curb to my right an elderly lady caught sight of the pointed pixie cap which was all that she could see of the tiny Viki. Grabbing the arm of her gentleman friend, she smiled and nodded toward "the cute baby." He burst into a grin also, and then we were all nodding and smiling at each other. Suddenly Viki shifted in my arms and turned her chimpanzee face straight at the couple. I had one quick impression of their mouths falling open. Then the light flashed green and we moved on.

We were alone for the next few days while Grandma went across the state to visit friends at St. Petersburg and Tampa. She won some card games, and sat on the Green Benches where she picked up some amazing stories, but in a short time she returned. I suspect that there were too many old people there for her. During her absence we decided in conference that we were not doing right by either her or Viki. Our antisocial ape needed a long-range plan of social living, of getting used to all kinds of people in all kinds of situations. And since Grandma was already accustomed to that way of life, we now showered upon her and Viki rides, adventures, people, and a party almost every night.

Here in the first major instance, Viki demonstrated her ability to adapt to new conditions as she has so often since. Perhaps the invasion of throngs of strangers, perhaps having a semistranger in the house all the time lowered her resistance, for she began to play with her toys in company as relaxed as when we were alone. She began to run up and down the room once more, galloping on all fours. She would slap the bookcase, turn, run to the table which was the other terminal, swing around one leg of it, and race back to the bookcase. In quieter moments she played under the table, climbing over and under the chair rungs.

While Viki played, Grandma and I visited. Once more she told her wonderful stories of long-ago times and strange people while her knitting needles clicked out bootees for Viki. But it was hard keeping Grandma's mind on her yarns since it wandered constantly to Viki and her antics. "Look at that now. Just look at that," she would say as Viki paraded past with her shoulder purse slung around her waist and threaded through her legs so that it flopped behind.

When Viki grew tired she climbed onto the couch and threw herself down between us in the posture of a bored child. She rubbed her head against us irritably, and then with a yawn heaved herself into yet another slouch. Then Grandma would say softly, "I wish we could be friends, Viki. Please let me stroke your head, won't you?" And if Viki was sleepy enough sometimes she did.

I could see Grandma coming under Viki's spell. She began to watch the clock for feeding and pot sessions just as we did. She would interrupt a tale of St. Petersburg's Green Benches, where life apparently begins at eighty, to say, "Isn't it time for her to go on, dear?"

One day after a drive I was shocked speechless when Grandma picked up Viki's elfin cap, and turning it over tenderly in her hands, said, "I must send Viki the little bonnet Keith had when he was a baby."

As Grandma was amused, then enchanted, and finally downright fond of Viki, so the little ape relaxed her earlier opinions of Grandma. In a pattern of getting acquainted from which she has never deviated, Viki first smelled the visitor's shoes, then her clothes, and then she examined Grandma's hands very minutely. She started to accept bribes of orange pieces and mints. Grandma discovered that she could extract one of the big chimp grins she came to adore by dancing the monkey doll before Viki's face. Viki, in turn, practiced bluffing for the first time, a fine art in which chimpanzees need no practice. As she descended upon Grandma's ankles with her mouth wide open, Grandma squealed in mock terror. With the dominance hierarchy thus established, the more Grandma retreated, the bolder Viki grew. She would lunge at first one and then the other matriarchal leg until she had Grandma hopping all over the room.

At six months of age Viki was earning her food on the string problem. Seated in her table, she got her milk by pulling the correct string of a pair, one of which was tied to a little cart holding the bottle, the other unbaited. She was doing fine until we discovered the secret of her success. No matter if the strings were parallel or crossed, the weight of the bottle told her which one to pull. Just before Grandma came, we had added a wooden block to the heretofore unbaited string, thus equalizing the weight and thoroughly confusing Viki. Now she was compelled to *look* at the ends of the strings before she knew which one led to the reward. While Viki pulled strings,

Grandma pulled for Viki. If Viki chose correctly, Grandma cheered. If Viki cried because she made a mistake, Grandma sputtered indignantly at making such a little thing work so hard. One day in a spontaneous burst of insight Viki pulled both strings at once, thus insuring a reward. Grandma nearly burst her stays laughing at our frustration.

"Well, she hasn't won, you know," we protested. "We will just put the strings farther apart. We won't let her take two at once." But Grandma kept on laughing.

Grandma's visit ended all too soon, but for Viki its effect lasted forever. Never again did she fear people in general. From her six-month birthday she grew more sociable, even dependent on people, until today Viki is at her best in the company of human adults.

I remember Grandma's visit as a pleasant time, a brief moment of gracious family life. But with her little suitcase in her hand, Grandma does not linger over leavetakings. She breezed out as abruptly as she had burst in with her memorable question: "Where is that creature?"

Now, her last words, as Viki and I waved from the doorstep, were, "Hurry inside, dear. You don't want the baby to take cold."

CHAPTER 5.

Under a Spreading Pecan Tree

SOON after Grandma returned to the wintry North, spring came to Florida in earnest. The balmy air fluttered the feathery new leaves on the pecan trees, and in the mornings, chiffon mists floated in off the marshes. Along the highway wild berries ripened, and the roving pigs which feasted on these delicacies crossed the cattle guard for choice berries inside our fence. One day Viki and I went out to examine the first spring flowers in Mrs. Clarke's garden, and found that we did not want to go back inside. From March until November we used our house for little more than sleeping.

Under an especially luxuriant pecan tree in our yard stands a large wooden swing, suspended by chains from a metal stand. When we discovered it, the metal parts were corroded with rust, and the wood was dry and weathered. No one had used it for years, but Viki immediately claimed it as her own. While I sat in the middle of the swing, reading, she ran back and forth on all fours, merrily climbing over my lap. In time I learned to raise my book at the exact moment she approached on the run and to lower it slowly behind her. Our movements became so well synchronized that she never missed a step and I scarcely skipped a word. As she grew more at home on the swing, however, she began to grasp the chain supports, lift her feet, and kick out into space, or more specifically at me. At this point I moved to an adjacent lawn chair.

Gradually Viki learned to climb up the supporting chains until she reached the crossbar of the metal stand. There she dangled by her hands, six feet above the ground, looking much too small to be doing that sort of thing. Now she grew suddenly bold, and hanging by one hand, she slapped the adjacent pecan tree. Then, as if surprised for a moment at her own daring, she scurried down and snuggled in my lap. But before long she was up again, hanging by one arm from the crossbar, pivoting her body half a circle to the left, half a circle to the right, and slowly back. Occasionally she dropped lightly to the ground to chase a butterfly or a lizard, but she never left the swing for long.

While I watched Viki play at being a chimpanzee, I scratched the bites I was receiving from a great variety of insects. For her part, Viki showed no signs of being bitten by the creepy crawly ones, although she pestered them constantly. She poked twigs into the ant holes. She played pat-a-cake on the home of the mud dauber wasps. Bending over from the waist with her diapered bottom saluting the sky, she urged along waddling beetles with one long finger or with her lips brought to a point. At dusk we watched the lily leaves become lined with grasshoppers, who are said to dislike sleeping on the damp ground. Viki, with budding gourmet tendencies, plucked a few of these each afternoon and chewed them solemnly, spitting out the tough exoskeletons.

Out under the pecan trees, we became acquainted with the many forms of animal life besides our own which inhabit the Grove. There were squirrels as big as rabbits, rabbits as big as dogs, and an ancient turtle who crashed through the brush with more noise than the neighbor's biggest brood sow. Of all the critters, Viki was most fascinated by the birds. She ran after them, not once attempting to seize them—though she often had the chance—but only to watch them soar into the air. Sometimes as they took off, she held out her arms and did a graceful falling pirouette as children do in imitating airplanes.

During rare quiet moments she sat on her swing, turning the pages of picture books, or examining her monkey doll's button eyes. She was beginning to notice more and more of her environment. Every passing car or airplane, every person who came in sight, any sudden sound or movement caught her attention. When the pigs came to devour what the bugs had left of my garden, she always noticed them before I did and clutched me in warning. Then, with her a-straddle my hip, I would grab my trusty BB gun and run them from the Grove.

One day on the swing Viki suffered her first wound. She skinned a finger between the slats of the swing. I washed it, applied iodine, and then unthinkingly sympathized with her. Apparently I overdid my concern for she began to "oo oo" so loudly and worriedly that I wondered if we would be able to save the arm. Chimpanzees never shed tears, but they have no trouble at all in expressing unhappiness.

With the finger swathed in bandages we returned to the swing, where she resumed her gymnastics, holding the finger out stiffly. Every so often she plunked down to stare at it. After her nap—during which the bandage fell off—she was seemingly recovered, until I examined the wound. Then she held it out tenderly and cried, "Oo oo, oo oo, oo oo," very much the invalid.

Viki continued to develop her motor skills. While Grandma was visiting us, Viki had discovered that she could stand upright by herself. She had pulled herself to standing against a

table leg and then let go. She teetered there for a second before falling lightly to her hands. She was so delighted that she
went from chair leg to table leg to door jamb all over the
house, pulling herself up and letting go.

One day while holding her big ball in one arm, she pulled
herself to standing with the other. Now both arms went
around the ball, and she ran upright for three rapid steps,
clutching the ball tightly. She followed this routine thereafter
until the ball became an integral part of her walking. Then, to
her great delight, she discovered that she could walk upright
empty-handed. Holding out her arms for balance, like a child
walking a fence, she toddled along, a great big grin on her
face.

While upright locomotion was fine for short jaunts, or the
last few steps before reaching a goal, distances of more than
three feet were still traveled in her swift quadrupedal gait
which sounded like the gallop of an extremely small horse.

After little children learn to walk they soon discover the
thrill of pulling toys behind them. One day in May Viki took
my hand and began to pull me so that I became her first pulltoy. I followed obediently as she led me to the door. I opened
it, and she slipped out, pulling me after her toward the swing.
When I held back, she took my hand in both of hers and
tugged until she fell over backward. In the days thereafter I
was at her mercy, spending much of my time under the table,
behind the radio, in the pantry, or wherever she led me.

Viki discovered yet another use for a mother. She had always
tagged behind me, grasping the hem of my skirt with her hand.
Now she began sitting on my instep and wrapping her entire
self around my leg whenever I started to walk. With her thus
attached I limped through the heat of the summer. A solicitous
passerby who saw me hobbling as I hung out the diaper wash
came over to ask what horrible ailment had stricken my leg.

"Hanged if I could figure out what that black thing wrapped around your leg was," he said, polishing up his bifocals.

Viki had first practiced the chimpanzee art of bluffing on Grandma. Now, as the last of her major motor skills arrived, new confidence swept away her fears, and she began to challenge the right of any other animal to walk the earth. Her first reaction to one of the Grove's many cats was to bristle and stand silently tense. As the hair stood up on her back, head, arms and legs, she seemed to become more massive, and rather terrifying on a small scale. Next she would slowly rise to her feet and stick out her chest. Then with a great show of bravado, stamping her feet down hard, waving her long arms, she would charge her enemy. The cats ran for their lives. She would chase them for a few yards and then gallop back to me, all triumphant.

Dogs did not always run, but seemed to be bewildered at this strange organism, which was somewhat like a child, but furry like a dog. She would advance just so far, waver for a second still threatening, and if the dog did not retreat, she would turn and race back to my legs. Clutching me, she would rock back and forth in what Keith calls "soaking up some security," and then try her bluff again. Should the dog advance so much as a paw toward her, her retreat became a screaming rout.

The bluff worked so well on lesser animals that one day when the mule was grazing in the yard, I was amazed to see Viki bristle, draw herself to her full height of twenty-five inches and head for it with an angry bark. The mule peered down at her in lofty scorn and then moved off in the unhurried way of mules. Unfortunately Viki took this for a retreat. I snatched her up almost within kicking range of its hind feet. (I am happy to report that today Viki has a decent respect for the mule's greater size. She is not afraid in any cowardly sense, merely cautious now that she knows discretion to be the better part of valor.)

The same bluffing approach was used with little children when Viki first met them. If they would take our forewarning to show no fear at her initial bluster, they had fun playing with a unique playmate. But most often they became jittery and Viki kept them on the run until their parents carried them to safety.

One afternoon when Viki was nine months old, a little boy named Tommy came to visit her. We were all excited about this meeting. Lately she had become quite friendly with all adults, and we were anxious to see if this would be generalized to children, but Viki had long since scared away all the children her age we knew.

Tommy was a handsome robust child of eighteen months, to all appearances her equal physically. He was an intelligent boy, perhaps sweeter than most little boys. He took one look at Viki and saying, "Baby! Baby!," he ran to hug her. "Baby" showed her teeth and slapped him. Tommy backed away, apparently reconsidering his classification. Then he smiled and reached out to pat her head. She scratched him. He picked up her ball and tried to distract her with a game. She slapped it away. He sat in her coaster. She pushed him out. He picked up her monkey doll, and that was just too much. Suddenly possessive, Viki snatched it away with a sharp bark. Then she scooped together all her toys and sat down emphatically on the pile. Tommy at last got the idea. He looked as if he might burst into tears. That was all Viki needed. She immediately assumed her King Kong configuration, pulled his hair, tried to bite him, and when we slapped her, she again sat down on her treasures and pouted.

The poor little boy kept saying hopefully, "Bye bye, bye bye."

Finally we went out to the swing, hoping that Viki would become preoccupied with her athletics and leave Tommy alone. When he made one final stab at being friendly, she grasped the chains, took a running swing, and kicked him in the face.

Tommy withdrew to his mother's skirt. There he carried on an unintelligible but spirited conversation, while Viki cavorted overhead, for she could now travel hand over hand along the upper support of the swing. This scene might serve as a portrait comparing Viki at nine months with a child not appreciably older. The two had been raised under similar home conditions: toys, teachers, and training. Yet here was Tommy sitting motionless, but chattering incessantly, while Viki ran and jumped and climbed without the slightest vocalization. In trying to compensate for her natural silence, we had already started special training aimed at teaching her to speak, about which more later.

CHAPTER 6.

A Great Year for Pecans

OUR summer days assumed a lazy soporific pattern. In the hot still mornings Viki tumbled on her swing while I sat reading, with an ear on the alert for snakes and a hand ready to swat presumptuous insects. Viki still enjoyed the bugs a great deal more than I did. When occasionally she presented me with defunct cockroaches, she obviously did not understand my lack of enthusiasm. One day I jumped up and squealed when an enormous bee buzzed me. I recovered my composure only to find her looking at me with a very disconcerting little smile.

Viki and I were alone all day long except for callers, but we were never lonesome. With her schooling, our household chores, and our heavy schedule of fun and games, we were very busy. As the summer progressed Viki became more alive and inquisitive while I found it too hot to bother about "getting things done." As a result we discovered each other on that pleasant plane where children who are eager to learn meet adults who are not too busy with their own affairs. Viki began to take me for frequent walks to points of interest in her yard. She spent more time in my lap, looking at picture books or superimposing her scribble on whatever I might be writing. For long moments she simply gazed into my face without comment.

During more active periods we enjoyed all the standard games—tag, peek a boo, an elementary pat-a-cake—but we preferred games of our own invention. One such sport neatly satisfied my creative urge and her drive to destroy and make noise. On the cement walk outside our back door, I would build a fine tall tower of blocks and Viki would proceed to knock it down, not in any wanton slam-bang way, but in the elaborate, premeditated manner of a dynamite handler. She approached the tower on the run, skidded to a stop just short of it, and very carefully circled one arm around the tower without touching it. Now she paused perfectly still for a full second. Then, wham! she closed in. As the tower toppled, she raced to safety, scattering blocks on all sides. From time to time she added little bits of stage business, all aimed at creating suspense, at forestalling the crash. Sometimes she waved her hands over it as if in benediction. Or she would pause with her head almost touching the tower and kick her heels into the air several times. She always laughed as she ran from the scene of the crash and I threatened to catch her. We played at this game by the hour.

Although Viki and I were staunch friends, I was not her only solace in times of distress. We discovered that Viki could be comforted and kept sitting on the potty by giving her a towel to hold. This was a great convenience, but as time went on, it became a nuisance. Everywhere that Viki went a towel trailed behind, clutched in one hand, a foot, or draped over her back. I had the cleanest floors and the dirtiest towels in Florida. I tried to sneak them away when she wasn't looking, but as she tired of her erstwhile toy and decided to move on, she always reached behind her confidently for her towel. If she could not feel it, she looked, and if it was not in sight either, she ran frantically around the room, searching for it. Then she grabbed my skirt and bounded up and down until I gave her a towel in self-defense. When we wanted a tape recording of her scream, we could think of only one sure way to evoke it. We put her on the potty, gave her a towel to hold, and then firmly took it away.

Parents invariably tell me of their own children's love of rags, towels, and such. One three-year-old we know has toted a baby blanket around for most of her short life. She apparently remembers the emotional beginnings of its appeal, and aptly calls it a "mommy." At social gatherings, eyebrows quirk when Joannie goes up to her flesh-and-blood mother and wails, "Where is my mommy? I want my mommy."

Not only towels, but rags, magazines, sprays of foliage, even the mops are used by Viki to decorate herself. A certain zoo director who is very compassionate toward all her charges has said that she resents the human practice of putting clothes on apes. It violates the dignity of the animals, or so she says. This may hold true for performing bears or hippopotamuses, but I do not think it expresses an ape's own wishes on the matter. During these sweltering July days when I tried to keep Viki cool by letting her go native, she repaid my concern by struggling back into the clothes I had just peeled from her. And one day as the mercury climbed past one hundred degrees in the shade, she draped a ten-pound woolen blanket over her back and ran up and down the dirt road in the hot sun.

Viki seemed completely unmindful of the hot weather in spite of her coat of thick black hair. She galloped around the yard, pulling up crab grass and boxing with weeds taller than herself. A new type of running appeared where the hands hit the ground together, the legs are swung between them, and the arms are brought stiffly forward again, like someone on crutches. She discovered a new toy, the outdoor water faucets, and a new manipulatory skill, how to turn them on. She was rewarded with great gulps of cool water, and sometimes un-bargained-for showers. But the largest part of every summer morning was still spent twisting and turning and flinging her-self about on the swing.

In the hot high noons we fled indoors to bathe, nap and give Viki her schoolwork. She had outgrown the kitchen sink, and in getting her accustomed to the great white expanse of the bathtub, I went into the tub with her at this time. The pro-cedure was to bathe her, rub her dry, and turn her loose in the living room while I finished my own bath. Viki's love of rags and her incipient sociability here led to a dire consequence. While I sat marooned in the tub, she would carry away all my clothes and maybe even the towels. Then perching atop the bookcase at her favorite window, she would wave my things at any folks who happened by. Naturally they came over to in-vestigate. Viki smiled and pounded and hooted her hello, while the visitors said, "Well, Ah declare!" or "Did you evah!" Since the bathroom opens only onto the living room, I was stranded until the party broke up.

If I was in any condition to receive callers, they enjoyed watching Viki at work on her problems, for while other little girls had summer vacation from school, Viki's afternoons were spent working at her studies. Actually, of course, these were presented as play and Viki worked at them in the spirit of a person solving fascinating puzzles. Since she had mastered the string problem, she was learning to speak for her food and this was serious business. But most of our work was mere child's play, the sort of child's play by which the human learns many things—how to open every type of container, how to use various gadgets and put things into other things, mechanical principles such as turning cranks and pushing levers.

Viki showed much interest and persistence in these matters for one so young, but she was easily distracted by the sight or sound of any activity outside the windows. If a car passed by, for example, she chinned herself on the sill, and watched it out of sight before returning to "school."

One hot afternoon Viki and I were resting in the comparative cool of our living room. She had just learned to use the latch on my handbag and had rewarded herself with my compact. She was sitting in the window in a stream of sunlight, patting the compact and swishing her long hands through the clouds of powder that arose. Suddenly she bristled and stared hard at something just outside the window. The next instant I heard the dread sound of a rattlesnake. I snatched Viki to me. Again came the hasty dry rattle. It was very near, but I could not see the snake. We stayed in the house until Keith came home. He set out with a bludgeon, but he found no snake, although we heard the sound many times. We told Robert about it, and the men poked around in the bamboo thicket and in the rock garden behind the lily pond. The snake was now silent, and they could not find it.

Viki and I were looking out the window about noon on the following day when I felt her body go suddenly tense against me. Then like a stab at my taut nerves, the rattle came again, this time right under the window. Viki slowly rose to her threatening posture. I stood perfectly still and watched her eyes. They were focused on the azalea bushes outside. I looked at the exact spot which had seized her attention and saw—a grasshopper!

But such a grasshopper! It was at least five inches long with a lovely lacquered body of gold and black. Toward the rear was a pair of beautiful red wings which were normally held tucked in close to its body. Now as I watched, these crackly little affairs began shooting in and out, in and out. They made a sound identical to a rattlesnake's!

In the summer evenings, Viki was exposed to a round of informal parties. Now she came into her own socially, and while she was very nicely behaved usually, there were a few little mishaps. One night she sat ever so calmly on my lap at a spaghetti party, and then unexpectedly took it into her head to spank the contents of my plate. Another time at a swimming affair, Viki, who abhors closed doors, became the life of the party by banging furiously whenever anyone shut himself into the bathhouse. From inside came harassed mutters, "All right! All *right!*" Then the person would emerge, hastily thrown together and thoroughly disgruntled, only to fall over this furry black mischief.

With the appearance of her entire battery of twenty baby teeth, we were faced with the very real problem of her biting. She had always gnawed on our furniture and threatened children, but now that her jaw muscles became stronger and she grew bolder, not even adults were spared. At a swimming party she was nuzzling and smiling at Dr. Austin Riesen, who has worked with baby chimpanzees and is thoroughly familiar with their ways. Everything was very pleasant until Viki leaned over in what Keith called "the friendliest possible fashion," and bit Austin's ear. It was the first time she had ever drawn blood. I was so amazed that I almost fell into the pool. A bystander who was with us but not one of us said, "That's a chimp for you—unpredictable."

The psychologists rushed to Viki's defense. Austin himself never stopped smiling. He said that there was obviously no malice intended; she had merely misgauged her bite power. Henry Nissen called it a "chimp kiss." He thought that she had started to touch her teeth to the ear gently in the affectionate way of her species, but being young and excited by the crowd, she had been unable to control the force of her bite. Keith observed solemnly that Austin must have "awfully tender ears."

As summer went into its fifth month it became very very hot. Even Viki who had previously seemed unmindful of the heat flopped down all spread out during the hot August afternoons and just waited. At about three o'clock every day the rain came with a rush like an approaching locomotive. Some days then turned dark and chill; sometimes, however, the sun kept shining, so that looking up at the sky, we could see bright drops of rain like tracer bullets. If Viki could manage to slip outside during the showers, she opened her mouth toward the heavens and captured the raindrops on her tongue.

With no let-up in the heat things began to assume a zany aspect. The ants, for instance, found a new delicacy. I found all my rayon finery in shreds and the ants bedded down in the dresser drawer. Mrs. Clarke offered questionable consolation. Florida ants never go near a dirty house, she assured me. They love clean things. You'll find them in your linens and sheets, she said. I hurried home. I found them.

A man called up the Laboratory to ask if any of the monkeys were loose. One was in his bed, he said. We counted heads, but no animal was missing. Pretty soon the man called back. "Sorry, my mistake," he said. "It was only a honey bear," and with that he hung up.

The heat was terrific.

One hard day I glanced up from my writing to see Viki on the couch soberly turning the pages of a book. It was Clarence Day's *This Simian World*. It became her favorite book, and one without which no primate's education is complete, but it rather unnerved me the first time I saw her engrossed in it. I went to the bathroom to bathe my fevered brow, and wearily upset a whole box of powder on the floor. Viki was delighted. She did a little chimp dance and tracked it all over the house before I caught her. No sooner did I get that mess cleaned up than Viki began screaming, but, to my distress, I could not find her anywhere in the house. She had opened a window and fallen out. I nailed the screens shut. The heat went on and on.

Viki made her own adjustment to the thermometer. Each time I opened the refrigerator for a coke, which was often, she crawled inside. This appears to be real genius, but in all fairness I must report a new game she now invented using her ever-present towel. Draping it over her head, she would run around the house like a small ghost, laughing as she bumped into furniture, until she sank down exhausted, her little face beaded with perspiration.

When we took our gripes about the heat to Mrs. Clarke, she merely looked as cool and calm as usual, and offered her philosophic opinion, "Well, it's been a great year for pecans, anyway."

CHAPTER 7.

Guess What Viki Did Today!

NOW that autumn had come to Florida, Viki and I again took to our yard. In the cool dry sunshine of October, we rested up from the summer, lazily watching smoke from bonfires twisting and blending into the gray Spanish moss. Robert began gathering in the first windfalls of a bountiful pecan crop. Viki greeted him from her swing, clapping her hands and stamping one foot in a great show of welcome.

The crisp autumn breezes were a delight to Viki. She opened her mouth wide and arched her tongue against the wind much as she reacts to a spray of water. These days she seemed to feel a new joy in just being alive. She became a skygazer, following the soaring hawks and the long-legged swamp birds as they streaked through the pines. Her keen observation of things around her was revealed in daily episodes. Once a small plane was cavorting in the clouds when the aviator suddenly cut his engine and went into a glide. It was a small plane and fairly high up, but the instant the sound stopped, Viki leaped into my arms and frowned up at the plane.

Viki at one year of age was not exactly the bookworm type,

preferring athletics to quiet play. She was now exceptionally beautiful, in a chimpanzee sort of way, and buoyantly healthy. In physical capabilities and neuromuscular control, she was definitely ahead of the child her age. Since it is the nature of chimpanzees to mature at a faster rate than humans, Viki had sat up unaided, stood alone, walked and climbed earlier than a child would have, at a ratio of about three to four.

On the Gesell tests of development Viki's performance was also superior to the majority of human "Ones," probably because both species are tremendously immature at this age, with the chimp having a slight edge physiologically. In the use and understanding of language she showed no serious deficit as yet. We did not learn until later that even at one year the human is receiving a great deal of language education, which will enable him by the age of three to rise far above the most intelligent of chimpanzees.

Tests gave us at best only a rough approximation of Viki's progress. Our personal evaluations have always been based largely on her problem-solving ability, her play behavior, and her social responses. Between one year of age and eighteen months Viki seemed to experience a "mental awakening." It was as if all our coaching and all her scattered bits of information were beginning to fit into a pattern which she could understand. These days, when she finally solved a hard problem of long standing, a look of sudden comprehension lit up her face in what some psychologists refer to as the "ah hah!" phenomenon.

As "proud parents" we began to torture our friends with a fine large collection of Viki stories. One day, for example, I was in the yard collecting pecans in a large pan. Since books on child-rearing recommend that the child be permitted to "help mother" I offered Viki her sand bucket and invited her to join me gathering pecans. She did not seem to see it my way.

With grand gestures I demonstrated the delights of picking up a nut and tossing it into the sand bucket. She resisted me. I pleaded with her and gave her a head start by transferring some pecans from my pan to her bucket. She only eyed her swing longingly. Then I became firm. I *ordered* her to gather pecans. "When your bucket is full, you can go to the swing," were my last words on the subject.

Feeling every inch the self-righteous parent I resumed my gathering. A little while later, with an apron load of pecans, I returned to my pan. Viki was bending over it with her hands buried under the nuts. Now, even as I descended upon her, she scooped up a double handful of nuts, carried them to her sand bucket, and dumped them in. Then off she galloped to the swing.

Whenever Viki flipped a light switch, she glanced at the ceiling fixture, which gave off light as a direct result of her manipulation. The switch next to the front door gave her no such satisfaction, however. It controlled the hall light, which was out of sight when the door was closed. One day Viki made a spontaneous adjustment to this problem, entirely of her own accord. She climbed onto a chair and flipped the switch. Then she grasped the door knob, swung down from the chair, and still hanging from the knob, peeked through the keyhole. She was by now on noisy friendly terms with the Blums upstairs, and if she missed greeting them when their car drove up, she contented herself with a glimpse of them as they passed the keyhole.

One day Viki was sitting on the potty waiting for the un- likely to happen. I sat on the floor before her demonstrating some mechanical toy. She rested her chin on her hand like a bored thinker. Suddenly she sat up straight and stared at something behind me. Her eyes moved up and down as if

sizing up a person. I turned, fully expecting to see that some
quiet visitor had entered our living room, but there was no
one. I tried to see what had caught her attention, a bug perhaps, or a spot of sunlight, but there was nothing new. "I can't
see anything, Viki," I said, slowly turning back to her. "What
did you think—"

But I was talking to myself. Viki had left the potty and was
playing behind the bathtub. There is probably some perfectly
simple explanation. Since she had never seen any Western
movies at this time, how could she possibly have known the
"look behind you" trick?

An old occupation of Viki's now emerged as an obsession.
As if suddenly discovering the power of the written word,
Viki began to scribble on books, floors, walls, and furniture,
as well as the more orthodox paper. I found her comments on
assorted manuscripts, shopping lists, and on recipes I had
tacked to the kitchen bulletin board. Viki was not a tempera-
mental writer who insisted on a certain pencil sharpened to a
particular point. She wrote with screw drivers, crayons, the
sharp corner of a wooden block, and any old pencil—lead or
eraser end.

Her only claim to originality was her unique writing postures. In a frivolous mood, she stood on her feet and elbows
and steadied her paper with her chin, periodically kicking her
heels into the air gaily. For more serious works, she sat on the
floor with her legs stretched out before her and her body
between them, flat against the floor. In this case, she might
hold the pencil with both hands at once, and steady it against
her forehead for good measure.

Another behavior pattern appeared at this time, the significance of which is not for us to say. We think that it may have
been her budding awareness that the world is a strange and

mysterious place. The first thing that seemed to inspire her with awe was a wall socket. Perhaps she had received an electric shock, for she had been playing with the cords and plugs. All I know for sure is that she sat down all of a sudden and stared wide-eyed at the wall fixture. Then she said, "Boo," a sweet muted sound made against the soft palate. For weeks afterward she periodically plunked down to stare at this particular socket and utter her awe-stricken "Boo."

She was given a toy ukulele which she greeted not so much with fear as with wonderment. She watched fascinated when someone demonstrated how it was played but she refused to handle it herself. Finally we threw it into her coaster in disgust, and it lay there silent and forgotten. Several days later I was surprised to hear three notes struck upon the ukulele. Glancing up, I saw that Viki was standing upright beside the wagon. As I watched she reached out cautiously, flicked the strings, and said her mystified "Boo." Then on soft tiptoes she crept away. Not until she was several feet away did she burst into her usual manic activity. Many times we saw her approach the ukulele, tower over it wide-eyed, pluck a few notes, perhaps express her wonderment, and then steal silently away.

A natural sequel to her expanding mental ability was a greater flair for mischief. As she learned to put round pegs in round holes, she began to put odd bits of rubbish into my cooking. As she learned to pile blocks, she made towers of glassware, which was never intended for that purpose. As she was taught to get her food by pulling strings, poking with sticks, climbing onto boxes, she naturally generalized her accomplishments, and we were engulfed in a shower of tumbling lamps, pictures, and broken Venetian blinds. For this class of mischief I could not punish her with a clear conscience.

But there was the more serious nuisance of her biting. I discovered a scratch-removing polish with which to doctor the furniture, but I knew of no such remedy for bitten people. One day the worst possible thing happened. She bit *me*. I have repressed the circumstances. All I remember is that it hurt and something primitive flared in my blood. Grabbing her nearest part, a furry little arm, I bit down as hard as I could. She yelped and clung to me in surprise. I thought I would die of shame. It was not a thing I had intended to do, but it was done, and Viki never since has so much as threatened to bite me. This method is not to be recommended, however, for use on just any old chimpanzee.

That day was a very bad one in general, for she followed up the bite with some broken dishes, a nibbled lampshade, and finally she ripped the sleeve out of my favorite housecoat.

That night Keith and I had a conference. "The instant she does something like that, she should be punished," he decreed.

"But *how?*" I asked, not merely because I am chicken-hearted, but because this is a real problem with a chimpanzee. Her skin is tougher than ours, and cushioned with hair, so that when I slap her, she generally laughs as if I am tickling her. I refused to use a weapon. Since a child comes equipped with buttocks, spanking seems the logical thing. But a chimpanzee child's bottom is hard and bony with no fleshy pads. I am genuinely concerned with the orderliness of a universe where such a mischievous little hellion as a baby ape is provided with no spanking area.

"She's into one thing after another all day long," I cried. "She's bright enough on her problems, but if I didn't quiet her down now and then, she'd simply run about and climb and nothing else."

"Well, she's hardly more than a year old," Keith reasoned, and added a far-fetched tale about a time when his greatest expenditure of energy was in a game called Cops and Robbers.

But I was too disturbed to be comforted. "Oh, Keith, maybe she will always be rowdy like this and never learn to obey. Maybe she will never enjoy quiet games." And then, forgetting my numerous evidences to the contrary, forgetting her performance in school that day, I whispered the most horrible doubt that a couple of psychologists can have about their child: "Maybe she's not as intelligent as we think she is."

Nothing further could be said. We sat in the gathering gloom, feeling like a pair of heretics with no great confidence in our heresy.

At this point Viki who had been busy in the bedroom opening and shutting the windows, came to see what all the silence was about. She walked over to me, and resting her chin in my lap, searched my face with soft, questioning eyes. Then she snuggled into my lap and pulled my arms around her. She rested there a second and then switched on the lamp next to my chair, pleasantly brightening the room. Next she carried her hurdy-gurdy to the top of the low bookcase where she sat in the blue twilight lazily cranking out a tune. Down the road toward town a freight train trundled by, sounding the plaintive wail of Southern trains. Viki hooted a soft reply. Then she lowered herself to the floor and began fumbling through the contents of her small suitcase. She came up with a pencil and then her leather notebook. With these she climbed back into my lap, where she sat scribbling contentedly. Keith and I avoided each other's eyes and we never again discussed the frightful thing I had said. In a few minutes he went to the Laboratory for a good night's work while I made a firm but very very gentle stab at putting Viki to bed.

Viki was obviously absorbing a great deal from her environment, and yet we honestly did not consider her serious competition for the Quiz Kids. We merely thought that she was a

naughty but nice little chimpanzee girl. We frankly adored her.
We considered her quite clever, but felt that any number of
Laboratory baby chimps, brought up in this way, would turn
out much as Viki had to date. As modern parents do, we preferred to think of her as normal—"a perfectly normal home-
raised chimpanzee." And now at fourteen months, in her course
of development which had always approximated that of the
"normal" human child, Viki spoke her first word.

CHAPTER 8.

Teaching an Ape to Talk

OUR experiment had been born of scientific curiosity. We had wondered why apes do not learn to talk, since their vocal apparatus is similar to man's, and since they are able to learn many tasks which are seemingly more difficult than speech. The art of language cannot require very much intelligence, we argued, considering that the human child of one year is already beginning to master it. Why should not an ape, raised in a completely human fashion, acquire human speech? One scientist has marveled that deaf, dumb, and blind children have been taught by "beings they could not see to use language they could not hear." Surely an educated chimpanzee should be able to do as well, we reasoned.

However, while many people have reasoned that apes *should* be able to speak, the literature reveals very few apes who have done so. It is reported that a chimpanzee named Peter who was performing on the stage at the beginning of this century was able to say "mama" on command. A decade later Dr. William Furness, after months of hard work, taught an orangutan to say "papa," and later "cup." These two cases only served to sharpen our curiosity. Why couldn't we teach an ape enough language to communicate its needs and feelings? Why should this not happen easily and spontaneously under the proper conditions?

Viki came into our lives with the usual vocal repertoire of a baby chimpanzee. Although she never cried like a human infant, Viki had two sounds to indicate degrees of distress. She had a shrill scream for the worst possible thing that could happen to her—losing her hold and falling. For any lesser terror she protruded her rubbery lips into a funnel shape and said, "Oo oo, oo oo," apprehensively.

At one week of age, she said, "Uh uh uh uh," to anyone who bent over her crib. Sometimes this greeting came like breathy panting; again it was as explosive as a scolding. At five weeks of age she gave her first "chimp bark" when someone tried to restrain her. It was a sharp "rhow!" not unlike the bark of a small dog. She thereafter used it to express surprise or anger. At fourteen weeks of age she began making chimpanzee "food barks." When she mildly anticipates approaching food, the barks are indistinguishable from her greeting sound, but if she is really interested, the food barks become a staccato stream of "e's" (as in wet), the lips drawn back over the teeth.

All these sounds are standard chimpanzee vocalizations. They are instinctive, appearing in all chimpanzees, and persisting into adulthood with little change. Proof that they are inborn lies in the fact that they appeared without coaching in Viki, who had been raised apart from the other apes. These sounds are called up automatically when the animal is emotionally aroused and are no more under control than the knee jerk reflex. In fact we have come to designate them as Viki's "reflex sounds." Since Viki was being constantly stimulated by the attentions of the experiment, and since her reflex sounds burst out in response to this excitement, she probably made more different sounds than the human infant until the age of three months. So far the baby has only cried, with perhaps a few "coo's" of satisfaction.

At about three months, however, a remarkable thing happens to the human baby. Without apparent provocation, it begins to make sounds with its lips: "m's," "p's," and "b's" combined with vowel sounds like "oo" and "ah." Then, obviously delighted, the baby begins to play with other syllables. The stream of chatter grows more varied and more frequent. Driven by an undeniable urge, the child chatters almost constantly. His babbling includes not only the syllables of his native language, but all other known languages as well.

The importance of babbling as a basis for human speech probably cannot be overestimated. To the onlooker, the babbling baby is obviously having fun, but at the same time he is learning to use his lips, tongue, and breathing in different combinations. He is gaining control of these until in time he will be able to produce whatever sound he pleases. He is developing *the motor skill of vocalization.*

When the human is about five months old, he begins repeating his simple syllables and may say something like "mamamamam ma mah!" or "dadadada da!" Hearing this, his parents are overjoyed and proudly celebrate "Baby's first word." In response to the attention it gets him, Baby may repeat the word many times, although he will not know what it means until months later. It is here that the deaf child, who has been babbling, becomes mute—when further learning depends on listening to himself and grownups.

The normal child learns many words by hearing people speak. By receiving praise for only certain sounds, he concentrates on his native tongue and abandons the incoherent hodgepodge of his early chatter. This then is how a child learns intelligible speech and the whole long hard struggle has its beginnings in the play behavior called babbling.

Apes do not babble—at least not much. As an infant, Viki lay in her crib perfectly silent. If we spoke to her, she made her greeting sound and various monosyllables as well: "poo," "pwah," "bra," "bee," and "wha," but as soon as we went away, she fell silent again. This was the first sad fact we had to face in trying to teach an ape to talk: They babble very very little.

Once she said "ee oo" without provocation, and repeated it several times, apparently enjoying the sound of her own baby voice. At other times she played with "ah ho" and "ba hoo" or simply gargled a bubble of saliva to form a continuous "k." We were delighted and immediately drew false hope from this. Soon Keith's first question every night was "What did Viki say today?" And I would recite the "ah goo's," "pee oo's," and "coo ee's." Some days I had choice stories to tell, about Viki challenging her echo in Mrs. Clarke's spacious living room, or how she addressed a gathering of visitors with a stream of "uuh uh's" so varied in volume and inflection that everyone insisted that Viki was "talking."

But suddenly at four months of age Viki's spontaneous chatter fell off sharply. She still made the chimp noises with which she had come equipped, but we heard less and less of her "babbling," which had never approached the human level in either quantity or variety. Now, at an age when the human child begins making every conceivable sound, Viki grew increasingly silent until in the evening, when Keith asked me what she had said during the day, I found myself replying, "Nothing at all."

There were a few encouraging little flare-ups, like the day she went Hawaiian with remarks like "ah ha wha he" and "ah wha he o." But these exceptions only made the next day's silence more discouraging. Finally the only unprovoked vocalization we heard was a baby-soft "goo ah" as we tucked her in at night. It was so wistful a sound and so small a remnant of her earlier promise that it broke our hearts to hear it.

At this point we realized that Viki would not learn to speak by herself. She would have to be taught by the same methods used when children for one reason or another do not learn to speak naturally. We would literally have to put words into her mouth by shaping her lips and tongue with our fingers to form the various syllables. In special schools throughout the country, speech-handicapped children are thus helped to a more satisfying life. The teacher manipulates the child's mouth parts, demonstrates exhalation of breath, and lo! the child says "ma," "pa," "ee," "oo" or whatever. There are other techniques, including one in which the child watches the teacher's mouth and his own in a mirror and imitates her movements. All methods are long and tedious, but great success often results.

Since Viki's vocalization had become so infrequent, we decided that before starting her training in specific sounds, we would do well to give her some practice in making any sound at all on command. And since it has been suggested that apes lack an "urge to speak," we supplied that urge in the form of food, the standard lure for which Viki had been working all her life. From now on Viki would be required to vocalize for her supper much as a dog is taught to "speak."

She was five months old the day I first held out a portion of milk and said, "Speak!" She looked at the milk, and then at me, and of course said nothing. I waited for fifteen minutes and then rose to leave. As I moved away, worried little "oo oo's" broke the silence and I quickly rewarded her for making the sound. The milk tasted good and Viki sputtered food barks which earned her a few more portions. Then as her appetite wore off, we spent more long moments gazing at the food and each other. I kept saying "Speak!" and Viki kept saying nothing, but each time I rose to leave, she cried, and thus she earned her supper.

Viki was not really speaking *on command.* We were tricking noises out of her by arousing her emotionally in a way which automatically calls up chimpanzee reflex vocalizations. We hoped that in time she would see the connection between making sounds and getting fed, and would then speak of her own free will in order to get fed more quickly. We became very ingenious at making her "speak." We got food barks by stirring the food vigorously, by letting her smell it, and by pretending to eat it ourselves. A sure way to draw her worried "oo oo's" was for me to start leaving the room, a cause for great anxiety since my presence was as vital to her as food at this time. Once Keith and I fed each other until Viki cried for fear that she would get nothing at all to eat. Thus for five discouraging weeks we struggled to make Viki "speak."

Suddenly one day when she was ten months old, she began making a very strange new sound. The first time we heard it we were surprised and vaguely displeased for it was an ugly sound, hoarse and strained. It was like someone whispering "ah" as loudly as possible and with great effort. When Viki said it her face contorted while her eyes assumed the tense preoccupied stare of a stutterer. Then from her lips burst this rasping, tortured "ahhhhh." She then confidently reached for the milk, so that we concluded she had at last gotten the idea of speaking for food. From then on, whenever we told her to speak, she replied with this straining "ahhh," and we came to call it her "asking sound."

Why was it so terribly hard for Viki to make this sound? As we pondered this question, and re-examined our notes on

Viki's "speaking" for food, we realized an astonishing fact. Before our coaching *Viki had been completely unable to make any sound at all on purpose.* She made chimp noises, yes, but these were *beyond her control.* They were merely reflex expressions of her feelings. If she could have uttered even these voluntarily, she would have spoken up more quickly to get her food. As it was, she had to be disturbed before these burst out, and except for the chimp noises, Viki had been voiceless!

Why was Viki unable to vocalize when she wanted to, when her supper depended upon it? Perhaps because the ape, for all its humanlike vocal apparatus, lacks the neural organization necessary for voluntary speech; perhaps because she did not babble; perhaps some interdependent combination of the two was responsible for Viki's shortcoming. In any case until now she could not vocalize on purpose. She had lacked *the motor skill of vocalization.*

Now that Viki had this single voluntary utterance, the "asking sound," she used it in many "asking" situations besides meals. She asked to be gotten up in the morning, to be taken off the potty, to be given a towel out of reach, and apparently just for fun. She vocalized thus while doing other unrelated problems. One day while she sat on a chair and I sat on the floor, she said "ahhhh" for one toy after another as I held them up to her. Finally she was completely surrounded by toys. Then she seemed to realize that she had been taken advantage of. With a big saucy grin, she pushed the whole pile down upon me.

Now we were ready to give Viki some words. All we needed to do, we said blithely, was to hold her lips in the proper position, tell her to speak, and out would come human syllables. We hesitated for four more months hoping that her asking sound would become easier for her to make and for us to listen to, but since it did not change, we decided to get on with her first word. We chose "mama" because this is a very primitive sound. It is frequently the child's first word, and some variation of it is an almost universal designation of the female parent. Also it is easy to manipulate the mouth to form an "m," nothing more than pressing the lips together and then releasing them while the subject says "ahhh."

When Viki was fourteen months old Keith began this training at her morning meal. Holding her on his lap, he slipped his hand around her head so that his thumb was on her upper lip and his other fingers cradled her chin. In this position he could work her lips open and shut to form the m. Then with the portion of food in his other hand and Viki in her early morning hunger, he would tell her to speak. As she made her asking sound, he pressed her lips together and apart, and she said, "ma, ma."

She soon got the idea and began to inhibit her asking sound until Keith's fingers were on her lips. If he was too slow in getting ready, Viki often took his hand and put it in the helping position. Then looking up at him, she would strain her lips forward against the manipulating hand and say her "mama." If she was really hungry the word came out fiercely with a thrust of the head. One of our friends commented that this was the first time he had ever heard "mama" said like a cussword. As her hunger decreased at the end of each session, she leaned back on Keith's lap with her taut little tummy in the air and grinned lazily.

In a short time Keith became aware that her lips were moving under his fingers, forming the word by themselves. He stopped helping her then, although he did not yet remove his fingers. Instead he gradually moved them around to the side of her head until only the tip of his index finger was touching her upper lip. Finally even this was removed, and one morning, only two weeks after the mama training started, Viki said her first unaided "mama."

CHAPTER 9.

Enter the Stick

A CHIMPANZEE who can say "mama" is received into the community in much the same manner as a two-headed calf. In a very short time Viki became a public attraction. Friends, neighbors, Mrs. Clarke's pecan customers, and psychologists from the Laboratory came to hear with their own ears what someone prematurely referred to as "the talking ape." For a small consideration, a raisin perhaps or a bit of cookie, Viki said "mama" to one and all. Sometimes her word burst out emphatically, sometimes it was too soft to be heard, but in character it remained the same as when she had first uttered it. We could duplicate it by saying "mama" in a loud stage whisper.

The last step in our instruction had been touching our forefinger lightly to her upper lip. Now Viki "aided" herself in this way. Her finger did not actually move the lip at all—if we held her hands she did equally well—but perhaps from superstition, she preferred to touch her finger to her lip as she spoke her word.

As yet she did not know that *I* was "mama," but she had

many other uses for this new "asking sound." She awakened us each morning calling hoarsely from the depths of her crib. She begged for her food with this valuable word and to be extricated from each day's many crises. She even said "mama" plaintively when she wanted to be taken from the potty.

While Viki perfected her first word, we introduced other problems aimed at giving her control of her speaking apparatus. Since many sounds depend on being able to exhale a puff of air with the tongue and teeth in a certain position, we tried to teach Viki to blow. This proved harder than we had expected. We could not convey the idea of blowing a whistle by demonstration alone. When we put the whistle in her mouth and pressed her stomach or chest, it did not cause her to exhale but to inhale sharply. We bought soap bubble pipes, but Viki only sucked in the soapy water and soap became a favorite food. As to blowing into a glass of water through a straw— well, this is how we inadvertently taught Viki to drink through a straw. Not the least of our problems was that the little ape chewed up all the blowing equipment—feathers, windmills, balloons, and whistles—before we could give them a fair trial.

Viki had never lost her infantile habit of putting everything into her mouth. As with most chimpanzees, her big flexible lips are as useful to her in examining objects as are her hands. Unfortunately, mouthing and biting had become synonymous to Viki. As I fussed about her biting, most people charitably reassured me that their children had also passed through a biting stage at eighteen months to two years of age. They said that she would outgrow it. Hoping to hurry her through this embarrassing phase, I turned to the books on child-rearing for advice. They devoted long pages to explaining *why* the child bites. He bites to get maternal attention. He bites to establish dominance. He bites from "an overbrimming of love." He bites because a social situation is calling for a response, but he cannot think of anything better to do. While the reasons offered included everything but hunger, the recommended remedy was always the same: Explain simply and calmly to the child why it is *wrong* to bite.

I took Viki upon my lap and her big brown eyes paid me solemn attention while I talked to her. Then she gently placed the collar of my shirt into her mouth and bit a hole in it.

In recent weeks I had become discouraged about Viki in more respects than biting. Her strength and vigor coupled with restless curiosity and a slap-happy personality had always been a little hard on my clothes and household equipment. But up to now we had been philosophic about it, pointing out to each other that any child her age would create havoc occasionally. We simply kept laughing, lowered our level of aspiration, and survived. When visitors, seeing her leaping through the air and climbing up and down, up and down, asked, "How do you *stand* this?" we had explained that if you take a tiny dose of arsenic daily and gradually build up the amount, in time you can survive several times the lethal dose.

Yes, Viki had always been quite a houseful of ape, but I had never before doubted that we had her under control. Now, however, she began having temper tantrums. She refused to hand over forbidden objects, and if I was compelled to force them from her grasp, she went into a screaming fit, venting her anger on the monkey dolls by biting out hunks of their cotton insides.

When I gave the command "No! No!" she defied me. She stuck out her chest, made a sassy hooting noise, and returned to her mischief. If I slapped her, it made no impression on her. Sometimes she laughed and slapped me back playfully. It was clear that Viki had lost her respect for me, that she knew I could not really punish her, and that my "No! No!" was mere bluff. She acted like children I have seen who stamp their feet at their mothers, say "I won't!" and get away with it.

In work and play Viki and I were the best of friends, but in the matter of obedience she ran increasingly wild. On one occasion she opened a bottle of ink, and holding my shocked stare, poured it onto the carpet while I screamed, "No! No!" Another day she swung from the draperies which formed a makeshift closet, and as I closed in, she grabbed shoes from a shoebag and hurled them at me. Then she slithered down among the curtains, dragging all the clothes with her.

As I have done so often before and since, I took my problems to our ape expert, Henry Nissen. He did not see it as a problem in anthropoid behavior exclusively. In his quiet tactful way he pointed out that perhaps Viki's home life was a bit too easy-going, that perhaps no young animal of any species should get away with quite so much murder. Then he gave me his prescription: "Why don't you get yourself a little stick, and then when—"

"A weapon! I couldn't!" I protested so loudly that Viki sprang into my lap and clung to me anxiously.

"Oh, not a *weapon*," Henry said mildly. "Just a little stick with a sting to it. Then the next time she defies you, slap her just a couple times. That's probably all it will require to show her that you can back up your commands."

Reluctantly I cut a switch from a pecan tree. Then for several uncomfortable hours I waited, hoping against hope that Viki would not misbehave. But she did. She took my fountain pen from my purse and while I said, "No! No!" she uncapped it. I raised the stick and said "No! No!" once more. She put the point in her mouth and started to bite down. I slapped her twice across the shoulders. With a surprised "oo oo," she dropped the pen and wrapped herself around my legs.

I took her on my lap and showed her the stick, explaining the principle behind it. An hour later Viki was hanging from the blinds. When I told her to get down, she laughed and kicked out at me. When I picked up the stick, she got down. I could scarcely believe my eyes. Much of what Viki has learned has been at the expense of many trials, but in this instance she had learned almost immediately. She had apparently abandoned her idea of a mutiny without a struggle.

As time went on I was compelled to use the stick very seldom. Before long, simply wagging it at her or even the word "stick" brought instant obedience.

I was especially happy to have better control over her now that the schools were closing for the Christmas recess and people were coming to see Viki, bringing their children along. In addition to her own callers, Viki considered any friend of Mrs. Clarke's a friend of hers. To make sure that no one visited the landlady without also calling on us, Viki stood watch in the front window, banging on the glass to attract attention. Some people came to the front door, some to the back door, and if I did not answer immediately, they peered in the windows. She entertained them by dancing up and down on the window sill with her towel draped around her. If we were outside, she tumbled on the swing, or whirled round and round on the grass until she sank exhausted, her eyes still rolling.

With children younger than three she was gentle, but such meetings usually ended in tears as she upset the child with ever so slight a push. Her physical equals were now boys of six or seven. Unfortunately until this holiday, such youngsters had always been intimidated by her initial show of strength. And lately she had bit them at this quavering point. Now Jimmy Tarr, who was six, came into her life. Paying no heed to our advice that he proceed cautiously, he walked straight up to Viki as she stood on her swing and put his arms around

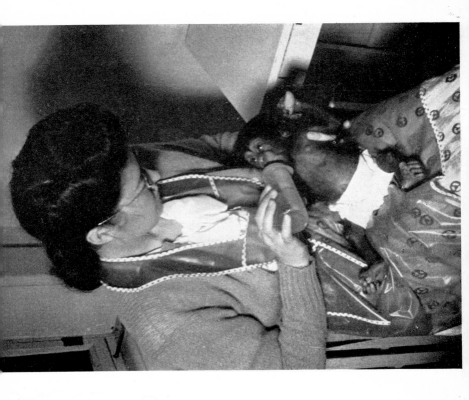

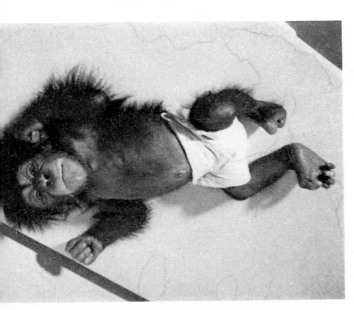

Viki at three weeks

Since three months of age Viki has been fascinated by mirrors

The "creature"—asleep in her crib

Bubble bath

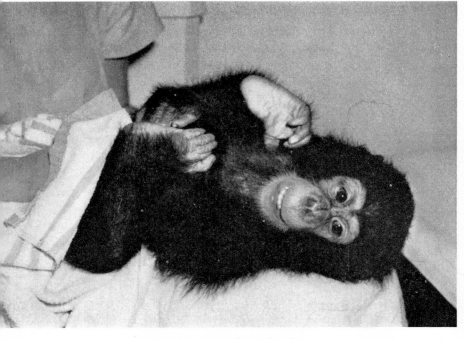

It takes three towels to dry her

Moving Viki's li[p]
form an m, as in "n[...]"

After two weeks, a touch
with one finger was sufficient

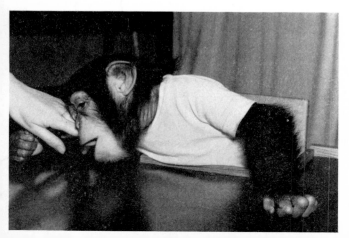

When we stopped[...]
ting our finger to h[...]
she put her lip t[o]
finger

her. I was too stunned to do anything. I closed my eyes and waited for his scream. When I had summoned courage to look, I was amazed to find that both Jimmy and Viki were smiling, and that Viki was also hugging Jimmy. Then there followed such a session of tag, wrestling, and peekaboo as Viki had never before enjoyed.

I watched nervously without too much faith in my control over her. But apparently I had nothing to worry about for now, although the future might bring problems of its own. When she began tugging too vigorously at Jimmy's sweater and I said, "Careful, Viki," she quieted down. When a car turned into the Grove and I called her, she was at my side in a second. Jimmy's mother commented, "She minds very well, doesn't she?" And I felt that I had already received the best Christmas gift imaginable.

CHAPTER 10.

Viki's Second Christmas

AFTER word of Jimmy's conquest got around, there was an epidemic of courage among Viki's young acquaintances. When children came to call, Viki immediately grew very excited and exhibitionistic. Sometimes her show-off tactics—slapping, tugging, and jumping at them from heights—threatened damage to the children. At these times I was always able to calm her down by speaking sharply, or by using the stick if necessary. In fact *I* was the only casualty of the holiday season. A three-year-old child was afraid of Viki so he bit *me*.

The question of baby sitters came up. Some of the youngsters told me that they earned money by baby sitting, and they volunteered to sit with Viki. I explained that we usually took her with us of an evening or on rare occasions left her home if we were sure that the Blums upstairs were planning to stay home. One insistent little fellow said that he got twenty-five cents for a weekly allowance and that I could have it if he could watch Viki when we went out.

Viki took an eager interest in all the preparations for her second Christmas. She licked the stamps which sent greeting cards on their way. To every gift-wrapped package was added the personalized touch of her teethmarks. Should holiday callers admire my cookies and ask for the recipe, I warned them that they might be unable to duplicate my results without a little chimpanzee to test the dough and poke her fingers in it.

As parcel post packages arrived, Viki was right in there supplementing our poky fingers with tooth and nail. She then draped herself in the wrappings and galloped about, trailing clouds of tissue paper. One of the earliest arrivals was a can of rum-flavored cookies which Viki welcomed with disconcerting enthusiasm. She stood upright, gazing wide-eyed at the delicacies, with one between each thumb and forefinger. I thought that I perceived a new reckless note to her food barks.

Grandma sent Viki gay red bootees for Christmas. Since store-bought shoes do not fit her hand-shaped feet, Viki was dependent for shoes on these custom-knit creations of Grandma's. She held one in each hand, staring at the bells on their laces. Then she tossed them high in the air, and kicked them all over the house with a fine merry jingle. Since they were too big, I turned up the toes like Persian slippers and sewed one bell on each turned-up toe. Besides being an excellent way to keep track of her, it provided a concentrated bit of holiday spirit.

As Christmas drew near, Viki's pile of loot became rather impressive. There were toys of all kinds, including a pulltoy and a monkey doll whose long tail qualified him as a pulltoy, too. There was a little banjo which she strummed with one end under her chin and the other end clutched between her feet. There were "educational" toys as usual, books, a pump which dispensed wooden balls, and a wagon full of blocks. All of these were immediately dragged along behind her by the pulltoy-minded Viki. There was a three-foot yellow plastic

Shmoo, which she clasped to her little self while she waltzed
across the room. To complete her haul, she received a new
mechanical toy, a cat which was motivated by having its tail
pressed down. She learned to do this quickly, and taking it to
the top of her bookcase, she pressed down the tail, and grinned
like an imp as it hurtled off the edge.

By the time Christmas actually arrived, each toy bore mute
testimony that it belonged to a chimpanzee. The Shmoo lay
collapsed, in desperate need of a patch. The monkey doll's
eyes were missing since Viki had bitten them off and was
carrying them about in her mouth. And the cat, surpassing its
quota of nine lives, had jumped from the cliff once too often.

On Christmas Day our house was filled with many callers,
much confusion, laughter, and the smell of food cooking for a
scheduled dinner party. Late in the afternoon it began to rain,
and during the let-up in callers, Viki and I bathed and dressed.
By now Viki was so devoted to her tub that, completely bathed,
dried, and dressed, she climbed back into the suds! Drying her
once more, I set her loose in the living room while I finished
my own bath. When I joined her, I found Viki performing on
the window seat. Outside in the rain, six little faces pressed
against the glass. Moisture had formed on the window pane,
and in this Viki was scribbling to the great delight of the
children outside.

At dusk the smell of roast duck became excruciating, and it
was time to set the Christmas dinner table. With a feeling of
elegance I spread the damask tablecloth. It hung over the sides
in graceful folds, which Viki proceeded to tug at. Next I set
up slim red candles which Viki bit into with ardent food barks.
I shooed her away from my table, and to avoid further trouble,
kept her in the kitchen with me until the guests arrived.

As the cars drove up, I took a last look at my table. The cloth
was white and magnificent. The glassware and silver gleamed.

The candles shed warm light on a centerpiece of roses. It was perfect. I opened the door and greeted my guests. The next moment they were all pointing at my table and shrieking with laughter. I turned in surprise. There, reclining across two place settings, was my errant chimpanzee, scattering rose petals where she lay!

The mama of an ape should know better than to have social pretensions. The tablecloth, for instance, proved to be only a nuisance, for the guests were compelled to lift the edges constantly to see what Viki was doing under the table. (She was mostly undoing shoe laces.) It was becoming obvious at these affairs that what we really needed was a glass-topped table.

After eating, we threw ourselves upon the sofa and chairs while Viki provided the floor show. She played "boat" in her cardboard box. She blew her whistle. (She had finally acquired this skill when we held her nose shut while pressing her lips closely around the whistle.) She played selections on her banjo, which had been reduced to one string, the others now serving as ropes with which to pull it behind her.

Viki was by now good friends with all these Laboratory people. As yet no one was allowed to pick her up or hold her hands, but this is no unusual social stipulation. I also make it, regarding myself. To each person Viki gave a selective reaction. She was quietly playful with mild Chow and ape-wise Henry Nissen, and rowdy with Bob Blum, who tickled her and generally appealed to her chimp nature. For instance, at this party he introduced her to a new sound which chimpanzees often use in play. It is similar to a "Bronx cheer" and is made by pressing the lips together tightly and blowing to form a continuous "pppppppp."

Later we had eggnog, and no one welcomed the change from the root-beer floats of her first Christmas more than Viki.

Once again parents were reassuring us. They said that children also like the taste of alcohol at two years of age, but cannot stand even the odor of it by the age of seven—in most cases.

As the evening wore on it became cold and we set up the electric heater. Viki did a pretty dance before it, warming herself. She looked like some primitive fire goddess as she slowly revolved, holding out her hands to the fire and raising her arms to warm her armpits.

Before I put her to bed I took her to the potty. She sat for a while and then stealthily crept back to the party. She bent way over as if to make herself smaller and clutched her towel for security. When I chased her back, she said, "Mama!" once, but was too sleepy to put up a fight. She turned, and returned to the potty, pressing her towel to her, and wagging her terminal tuft of white hair.

I put her to bed then, and with the life gone out of it, our party soon broke up.

It turned cold during the night, and as I tossed from too much roast duck and not enough covers, I became aware that Viki was restless also. Investigating, I found that the electric power had gone off, and that the heater in her crib was icy cold. Since she did not know how to keep herself covered, I saw no solution but to take her into our bed. There she wriggled and kicked, flinging her arms and legs every which way, until, in trying to escape from her, Keith and I were clinging to the very edges of the mattress. Then with the whole bed practically to herself, Viki began to whirl in a circle, corkscrewing the covers around her. In desperation I pinioned her down and said firmly, "Now, sleep!"

All was silence. She did not move a muscle. Then suddenly, right in my ear, she began to make loud Bronx cheers, backed up by hearty "mama's."

Keith sprang from bed with a start and also began to vocalize. Since I hold my position as wife more dear than that of mama to a "talking chimpanzee," I saw my duty clearly. I dressed her in a heavy woolen sweater and her heaviest bootees, and dumped her into her crib along with several blankets. She fell asleep immediately, and that was the end of Viki's second Christmas.

CHAPTER 11.

The Very Strange Case of
the Imaginary Pulltoy

THE singular events which I am about to relate find no parallel in chimpanzee literature or in the experience of my friends who work with apes. This story might better be told by a writer of detective fiction, or a psychiatrist, but since it must be told by me, only a bewildered mother, I shall tell it straight with no attempt to analyze, explain, or further confuse an already baffling mystery.

It all started on an unseasonably warm day in January. I was dozing over a book in the big chair while through the open bathroom door I watched Viki at play. She was supposed to be sitting on her potty, but while not yet completely trained, she always reaches the potty in time and so is permitted to play in the vicinity with her pants off when action is expected. She swings from the towel racks, bangs the door of the medicine cabinet, and snuggles into the wash basin. Most frequently of all she runs in circles around the toilet.

On the sunny afternoon our story begins, I sat lulled by the bird song and the sunshine when suddenly I became aware that Viki's monkey-jungle activity had stopped. She seemed to be absorbed in a brand-new game. Very slowly and deliberately she was marching around the toilet, trailing the fingertips of one hand on the floor. Now and then she paused, glanced back at the hand, and then resumed her progress.

"What are you doing, Viki?" I called, and was instantly sorry that I had. For she stopped short with a rapid look of guilt and embarrassment. Then she pretended to be very busy examining a knob which juts out from a pipe behind the toilet.

During the next couple of days Viki often played this new game, but now she paused frequently to make sure that I was not watching her. She has always practiced games on the sly, permitting no one to join her or even to watch until she has attained considerable skill or established the rules of the game.

Watching her cautiously so as not to be apprehended, I thought at first that she might merely be enjoying the vibrations from her fingertips as they scratched along the linoleum. But gradually I remembered where I had seen her act this way. Viki was at the pulltoy stage when a child is forever trailing some toy on a string, when everything with a string attached becomes a pulltoy. Dragging wagons, shoes, dolls, or purses, her body assumed just this angle. She trudged along just this busily on two feet and one hand, while the other arm extended backward this way to pull the toy. Viki had an imaginary pulltoy!

No sooner had I arrived at this amazing deduction than she interrupted the sport one day to turn and make a series of tugging motions. That is, they would have been called tugging had there been a rope to tug, which of course there was not. She moved her hands over and around the plumbing knob in a very mysterious fashion; then placing both her fists one above the other in line with the knob, she strained backward as in tug of war. Eventually there was a little jerk and off she went again, trailing what to my mind could only be an imaginary pulltoy. This incident had convinced me that my hypothesis was correct.

Still I was reluctant to believe what I had seen until Viki found a new game to play with her imaginary toy. She dearly loves to "fish." Standing on the furniture, she pulls up from the floor any plaything with a string tied to it. Now from the potty she began to raise the "pulltoy" hand over hand by its invisible rope. Then she lowered it gently and "fished" it up again.

As a mother I had to face it. Was this the beginnings of imaginative genius, or a budding psychosis? Imagination or hallucination?

Soon the movements took place all through the day, whether or not I was watching, with either hand or in either direction. She often transferred the "rope" to the other hand, and reversed direction as she ran. But it never happened except around the toilet.

Early in February the thing reached a climax in what was to date the oddest event of our life together. It remains in my memory as a symbol of the affectionate rapport between us and the tragedy of the language barrier which separates us.

It was one of those days when Viki loves me to distraction. All day long she had pestered me to hold her. She had pattered along in my shadow and cuddled close when I came to rest. At every little crisis she called for "mama," and was very much the helpless baby. Late in the afternoon I was combing my hair before the bathroom mirror while Viki dragged the unseen pulltoy around the toilet. I was scarcely noticing what had become commonplace, until she stopped once more at the knob and struggled with the invisible tangled rope. But this time she gave up after exerting very little effort. She sat down abruptly with her hands extended as if holding a taut cord.

She looked up at my face in the mirror and then she called loudly, "Mama! Mama!"

Suddenly I was frightened by the eerie quality of the whole business, but I felt that I must play along for the sake of our future harmony. I said with a smile, "Here, let me help you."

Acting out an elaborate pantomime I took the rope from her hands and, with much pulling and manipulation, untangled it from the plumbing. I dared not meet her eye until I held out to her the rope which neither of us could see (I think). "Here you are, little one," I said.

Then I saw the expression on her face. In a human mute it might have been called a look of sheer devotion, of appreciation for understanding. In addition a tiny smile played on her lips. And her whole face reflected the wonder in children's faces when they are astonished at a grownup's enthusiastic escape into make-believe. I have heard children say, "It isn't really true, you know. It's just a game."

But perhaps Viki's look was just a good hard stare.

In any event it was only there for a spellbound second. Then her funny little face crinkled into a grin and she tore off around the toilet faster than ever before, dragging her imaginary toy behind her. I just stood there, feeling very eccentric indeed.

After this I decided to get into the fun. One day as she played on the couch in a confusion of toys, I began to walk up and down the room, trailing a ghostly pulltoy of my own. But my toy had sound effects. It went "clackety clackety" on the bare floor, had to be hoisted onto the rug, and there it went "squush squush." In a little while Viki began to stare at me. She jumped off the couch and came running, not to me but to my toy. I stopped and she stopped also, at exactly the spot my invisible rope met my imaginary pulltoy. She stared transfixed and then uttered her awestruck "Boo!"

The final episode occurred the very next day. Once again I was pulling my toy across the floor while Viki played on the couch. She noticed me and seemed about to come down. Then she began to worry, flopping prone on the couch and rocking nervously. I went on walking, glancing back, and going "clackety clackety" and "squush squush." Finally her eyebrows came together in great anxiety and she cried, "Oo oo, oo oo," as distressed as I have ever seen her. When I passed close by, she made a flying leap into my arms.

Had she had enough of a good thing? Did she resent my usurping of her game? Was she frustrated by my unique ability to produce sound effects? Did she recognize that make-believe is fun for a baby, but dangerous in a parent? Or have I misinterpreted the whole mystery? I shall probably never know, for on that day the imaginary pulltoy disappeared from our home never to be played with again.

CHAPTER 12.

Viki and the Child

THE child at eighteen months, while he may be an enchanting little creature, is a relatively incomplete human being. His social perceptions are still quite primitive. He shows little desire to please, or to excel among his fellows, small sense of guilt, no interest in co-operative enterprise. The adults in charge of his education must use patience and ingenuity in dealing with him, since he cannot yet be reached by words and reasoning. He often understands what is required in a simple learning situation, but if he does not, explanations are of little value.

Though he is still a baby, he is already on his way to the elevated status of human adulthood. And of the changes which will soon take place, none will speed his education faster than his accelerated language development. In the next six months he may acquire as many as three hundred words, and will comprehend increasingly more of what is said to him. Since language has been Viki's most difficult problem, let us review her intelligence at this turning point, before the paths of the two species might be expected to diverge.

The standard portrait of a child at eighteen months fits Viki very well. Not only were her everyday interests and activities qualitatively the same, but on developmental tests for pre-school children, she was turning in results typical of this age. At the most recent testing she had solved the three-hole form-board. She built impressive towers of six or seven blocks. She could draw a straight line in imitation, changing to a scribble as the tester did so. She could feed herself with a spoon, inhibit forbidden acts on command, open doors, wave bye, bye, turn the pages of her picture books, and was showing some promise in washing and dressing herself.

These tests should not be accepted uncritically, of course, as a comparative evaluation of Viki. At this early age her faster neuromuscular maturation may have still been working to her slight advantage. And the child too had an advantage in the fact that test apparatus is constructed for use by human hands, not those of apes. In any case, "intelligence tests" for the very young are of rather questionable validity.

Play behavior in the informal home situation is probably a more adequate measure of a home-raised chimpanzee's intelligence. We had wondered originally if our subject would enjoy toys. Would she play like a child? Would she indulge in games, imaginative, creative, and social play? Our answer at eighteen months was a hearty yes. Her most recent attempts to draw us into her play took the form of teasing. One day as I sat outside reading, a fly kept tickling the back of my leg. After I had waved it away several times without looking up, I grew so annoyed that I snapped the book shut, determined to annihilate the pest. I caught my "fly" in the act. With a sly little grin Viki touched one finger lightly to my leg, and then looked up into my face, supposedly to enjoy my vexation. When instead she saw me watching her, she chuckled breath-lessly and dashed up the swing.

In her choice of toys she also closely resembled the child. She liked blocks, balls, cuddly animals, scribbling, bead-string-ing, and take-apart-and-assemble toys, such as the pyramid of colored rings. Her current passion was pulltoys, with picture books becoming a late favorite. Like children, she often rejected store-bought toys to select her playthings from the household equipment. Light bulbs became balls, and shoes were dragged about by their laces. Viki frequently played contentedly by herself, but with people nearby—as children at this age engage in "parallel play."

The child at eighteen months is just beginning to imitate the activities of the grownups he lives with. At about this time Viki also began "aping" us. She helped with the dishes in a very businesslike manner. She dug at her fingernails with a nail file, patted a powder puff over her face with startling results, and insisted on being given a dab of lipstick, which she smoothed on, as I do, with a little finger.

Often she imitated our motions with no idea of what she was doing. For instance, every morning she ran outdoors to pick up the newspaper. Seated on the couch, she would first open the paper wide, and hold it at arm's length as if to scan the headlines. Then settling back she would turn the upper corners a hand's breadth, one by one, as though she were looking for the sports page or the comics. Occasionally she would grin and open a page part way as people do when some fascinating tidbit catches the eye.

There is no doubt that in many ways Viki was similar to the human child of the same age. However, we were interested in differences as well as similarities. We hoped that by raising her with all the advantages of our culture we might discover the specific ways in which chimpanzee intelligence falls short of man's. When people saw the eighteen-month-old Viki, they said with varying degrees of shock, "Why, she's practically human!" We who knew her best were well aware of the falseness of this impression. Because of her education, Viki did have many characteristically human accomplishments, but there were already pronounced differences which were bound to place her at a severe disadvantage in the months to come.

For one thing Viki was extremely hyperactive. All children seem to be studies in perpetual motion to their parents, but there was no comparing Viki to the normal child. She ran in four gaits on hands and feet as well as walking upright when carrying toys. She jumped from heights three times her own. She sailed through the air from the top of the refrigerator to the top of the kitchen door, where she crouched like a recumbent leopard, watching me at work. While not yet climbing trees, she had begun to fling an arm or a leg over the branches which hung low over her swing. Her eyes seemed to be constantly glancing up, up, up, for a door jamb, a window casing, a human being, anything to climb.

We accepted Viki's three-dimensional way of life, interrupting her only when it became a matter of self-preservation. Meanwhile we began looking for a larger house to contain our growing ape. The only real harm in her preoccupation with athletics was that it took most of her time. If experience, rather than maturation, accounts for most intellectual growth, as we suspect it does, the comparatively quiet child is able to gain more cultural experience per unit time. We did not doubt that Viki was learning to be an excellent acrobat, but we were more interested in developing and studying her intellectual aspects.

A more important difference, one more apt to cause Viki to fall behind from now on, was language ability. At eighteen months a child commonly uses ten words; Viki was still struggling with her "mama." On the tests her only failures were in those items involving use of words or the following of spoken instructions. In the beginning we had argued that apes do not learn to talk because they are raised under such distressing circumstances. We pointed out that children in institutions very often have speech handicaps. We said that if an ape had a proper upbringing, it might learn to speak spontaneously. But we were wrong. You can dress an ape in the finest of finery, buy it a tricycle, and kiss it to death—but it will not learn to talk without specific training.

Having established language as her major shortcoming, we had proceeded in an attempt to overcome it by special methods. We had been working for the past month on a new technique with which we hoped to enlarge Viki's vocabulary. We would place her on the table before us, and then perform some simple act, such as clapping our hands or blowing a whistle, meanwhile saying, "Do this!" To get the reward (a jelly bean or a bit of marshmallow) Viki must repeat our actions. At first she merely stared at us blankly, and we had to put her hands through the motions. She picked up the idea quickly, however. At eighteen months of age she was able to "do this" in imitation of six different acts. She could blow the whistle, pat the end of the whistle as she blew it, clap her hands, pound on a can, draw a stick along a toy timpani, or put a wooden bead on a string, whichever task we demonstrated. Later we would introduce sounds and mouth movements into this "Imitation Series." Perhaps after enough sessions of "do this," Viki would be able to "say this" in imitation.

It is relatively easy to teach a chimpanzee stunts, but there was a purpose behind each stunt which Viki learned. Even the meaningless acts of the Imitation Series would in time provide her with a useful tool for solving problems, and for learning further words. A large part of her education concentrated on those stunts which every child learns under the heading of "training." We were introducing her to personal care, mechanical principles, and the constructive possibilities of various toys—the sort of things that eventually enable adult human beings to handle tools, drive cars, play musical instruments, and do similar high-class stunts.

Some of Viki's problems were designed both for giving her experience and for evaluating her abilities. One of the earliest tasks of her infancy, in which she pulled her bottle toward her by a string, falls in this category.

At thirteen months she learned that to get a cookie by the use of a small hoe she must place the hoe *behind* the cookie and rake it in. When the hoe was replaced with a plain stick, she instantly used the stick properly. She afterward used this principle in everyday life. Once, when a toy lay beyond her reach on the other side of the fence, she tore a switch from an azalea bush, and poked the toy toward her. In the final step of the stick problem, she was given two sticks, either of which was too short to reach the reward, but which were so constructed that they could be joined end to end to make one long stick. She had enjoyed putting sticks together like this as early as fifteen months, but she was not yet using the result as a tool.

In another of these problems, Viki was required to pull up a chair and climb upon it to reach a lure which was suspended from the ceiling. After one month of occasional practice, the seventeen-month-old Viki moved the chair under the lure without hesitation. Then she snatched her marshmallow so emphatically that the sticky string from which it hung flipped up and stuck to the ceiling.

We can be accused of "pushing" Viki, for we believe that by solving innumerable problems a man or an animal learns to reason, to attack each new problem in the light of past experience. According to Dr. Harry F. Harlow of the University of Wisconsin, a man unsurpassed in the art of working with monkeys, the formation of "learning sets" "transforms the organism from a creature that adapts to a changing environment by trial and error to one that adapts by seeming hypothesis and insight." His data actually show that animals gradually learn insight. In the same way, we believe that Viki is learning how to learn.

We were finding that Viki tended to solve each new problem with less difficulty than the last, and that we had to spend increasingly less time coaching her. A brief demonstration was enough to encourage her to exploit new objects for long minutes. As the normal home furnishes the human preschooler with endless stimulation, so Viki was daily absorbing new knowledge from her environment.

But what could we expect in the future? So far Viki's only intellectual deficit was language. What other failings would appear, to account for the cultural backwardness of her species? We could continue to give her a human environment, instruction, a wealth of personal experience, but would she prove capable of utilizing these? We faced the future with hopes, doubts, and a yet-unsatisfied curiosity.

PART 2.

The Second Eighteen Months

CHAPTER 13.

Viki and the Caged Ape

ONE of the oldest questions of human psychology is the nature-nurture controversy: Does a child mature into intelligence bit by bit as decreed by his heredity? Or does he *acquire* intelligence through experience in his social and physical environment? The answer is usually sought by comparing two children or two groups of children. We believed that by substituting a home-raised ape for one of the subjects and by equating its environment with the child's we would see the workings of a greater difference in heredity than exists between any two normal children. We have shown in actual fact that Viki's education caused her to resemble the child considerably at eighteen months. Those ways in which she differed could now be fairly ascribed to her anthropoid heredity. This was the first comparison we had set out to make.

Our experiment was designed to furnish yet another comparison: By contrasting Viki with a caged ape, we would have two animals with roughly the same heredity but with a greater difference in living conditions than any two humans experience. In what ways did Viki differ from other apes after eighteen months in a human home?

Viki's language deficit was conspicuous in the company of human children, but her one word already set her above her relatives verbally, and we saw no reason why she should not learn many more. She understood a great many commands also, and was receiving instruction in pointing to various objects, such as toys, her cup, and her whistle, and identifying parts of herself, such as her nose and ears. Whatever superiority she held in the field of language or language comprehension was entirely due to training.

Her play activity has been described as athletically "chimpy," and it is true that her gymnastics were quite like those of her caged cousins. But in addition, and again because of her environment, she played games with toys. She built simple block constructions, for example, and concentrated on mechanical gadgets. When we passed on her outdated toys to the Laboratory babies, they either feared them violently or ignored them. Even exploitation of toys is a *learned* behavior, and it is through playthings that the human child (and the home-raised chimpanzee) makes his first acquaintance with the mechanical aspects of our culture.

We cannot compare the intelligence of Viki and the caged ape by using the standard tests by which children and Viki are compared. The caged ones either fear or show no interest at all in the test equipment. All we can say is that in the use of the tools and concepts of our civilization Viki at eighteen months probably already surpassed the most experienced ape at the Laboratory. Her skillful use of faucets, switches, latches, sticks, strings and levers was once again a function of her environment, of her *acquired* intelligence. There is no reason to believe that her *inherited* mental capacity is unusually great.

Nowhere is the influence of environment stronger than in social education and the formation of personality. Laboratory babies of eighteen months are nearly always terrified of strangers. However, grown apes who have had the opportunity to see many people over the course of their lives beg visitors to notice them, to scratch their backs or tickle their tummies. This implies that apes, as well as people, must *learn* social ease. Viki, having been exposed to a great variety of social situations, was already infinitely less timid than her Laboratory contemporaries are, or than her jungle ancestors could afford to be. In this respect she was quite like other chimpanzees who have lived close to man. These are naturally gregarious animals; when deprived of the companionship of their own kind, baby chimpanzees bestow their love and dependence on their foster folks.

Viki was actually less of an introvert than the child usually is at eighteen months. She was full of happiness and smiles as she exploited each person according to his own inclinations, a tussle here, a nuzzle there, sometimes only quiet contemplation. She had all the bad traits of a child extrovert, too. She was a coquette, an exhibitionist, an opportunist, but all her tricks were aimed at her one great cause—getting people to notice her.

Certainly there is no more exacting yardstick of social intelligence than behavior at a large party. On Easter Sunday our director, Dr. Lashley, had a large party to celebrate completion of his new house, and we three attended along with perhaps fifty other well-wishers. Always the good mixer, Viki drifted among the guests with a pleasant grin and a gentle touch. Occasionally she patted a nylon or sniffed an interesting shoe but she engaged in no roughhouse and no biting. In fact, to my great surprise, one woman asked, "When does she get her baby teeth?"

Viki did start and stare at the first Easter bonnets she had ever seen, but they all went home sitting squarely on their owners' heads.

She nibbled at my food and sipped my drink, but she did not beg from strangers as she would have at home. My only tactical maneuvering was aimed at keeping her away from a plate of fudge which contained her two favorite foods, chocolate and marshmallow.

I had hesitated about bringing her into this home, where everything was either brand-new or antique, but as hard as she is on our things (which are neither new nor precious) here she behaved quite beyond herself. I remember her approaching one delicate little table which held several fragile dishes. She raised herself to standing with one hand poised as if to lean on the table. Then suddenly she drew back the hand and scampered off to rest on a more substantial footstool. Two young guests tried to attract her attention by playing catch with a pillow. She did not join them and when the pillow upset an ashtray, she ran to me, crying "Oo oo oo." Of course, she is not usually this well-mannered, and it is possible that she had caught our mood of self-restraint and awe at this shiny new house—which was also the home of our boss.

Like children, Viki tends to be contrary. At this party she tagged after our one colleague who can take young animals or leave them alone, and ignored completely the woman who was "just dying to squeeze her." After she had become very unhappy about Viki's snubs, the little ape went up to her sweetly and seemed about to give her a kiss. As the woman smiled at her tenderly, Viki's kiss turned into a raucous Bronx cheer and off she ran.

No trick of interior decorating can equal an ape as a conversation piece. I am always embarrassed by the way Viki monopolizes the conversation, but the questions which people ask are often stimulating and serve to clarify our thinking. A very provocative inquiry was made at this party: "What would happen," a man asked, "if you brought an ordinary cage-raised ape baby into this room during a party?"

When I had recovered from the shocking visions this called up, I answered that such a chimpanzee might race about the room wildly, knocking over everything, and screaming at an ear-splitting pitch. It might simply cringe in a corner, rocking back and forth nervously. It might attack everyone and everything in sight with tooth and nail. Our fellow Laboratory workers added their graphic bits to the picture until the man withdrew his question. He said, "I suppose it's all a question of how a creature is raised. It's only natural for Viki here to get along with people since this is the only life she's ever known."

The next morning Viki paid for her enormous intake of Easter eggs by being sick. Perhaps the generous swig of laundry starch with which she supplemented her breakfast had something to do with it. The person who took Viki's upset the hardest was Ruth, the big jolly woman who had recently come to work for us. She fussed and sighed over the prostrate little ape until about ten o'clock, and then, all at once, Viki was well and they were playing tag together. Her instant acceptance of Ruth into the household was a good example of Viki's ability to make friends.

The thing I liked best about Ruth was that she obviously considered Viki the most important member of the Hayes family. The first thing each morning she set all of Viki's toys straight and assembled our "school" supplies. Then she washed Viki's bed and table before even glancing at our part of the house. Viki's clothes also got first call. And in the course of her duties she never passed Viki without a greeting or a few minutes of play. Sometimes the thunder of their hide-and-seek was enough to drive me outdoors with a good book.

Viki in turn found Ruth a much more thoroughgoing housekeeper than I had been. Ruth insisted on a washboard for the small laundry, and the first time Viki saw this activity she was flabbergasted. She climbed up on the sink and watched closely while the woman soaped a garment and then rubbed it on the board. She kept saying "Boo" in a puzzled way and staring into Ruth's face, as if for an explanation. Then suddenly she joined in. She rubbed her own hand on the bar of soap, and up and down the washboard went her knuckles, rub-a-dub-dub.

Almost immediately Viki obeyed Ruth's commands of "No! No!" "Kiss me," and "Go to the bathroom!" But Ruth never changed Viki's diapers. As long as she worked for us, she was always going to do that "tomorrow." Viki strongly discouraged such intimacy.

Since Ruth had raised several children, she considered herself an authority on discipline. She frankly thought that Viki took advantage of me. Whenever Keith had spent a day baby-sitting while I shopped, Ruth could be counted upon to tell me frequently, "Dr. Hayes didn't have any trouble with her yesterday."

As consolation I told myself that Viki was still my baby and came to me when in trouble. One day she called "Mama" frantically from the swing. When I reached her I found no cause for anxiety. I asked her what was wrong. She immediately stuck one finger in and out of a loop of the chain. I examined the finger. It was still red and dented from where it had obviously been pinched in the chain.

So much for Viki's adjustment to people at this point. How did she differ from the caged apes in her reaction to animals?

Viki had visited the Laboratory several times. The older apes were curious about her, but she merely glanced at this assortment of chimps, the like of which no zoo can boast, and then busied herself with my hair and buttons. Up in the nursery the babies her own age drew back from her in terror, while she approached them with the same rough challenge she accords most children.

Although Viki preferred adult human beings, she occasionally made friends with young humans and the young of other species. Her newest friend was a mongrel dog who had wandered into the Pecan Grove and just stayed. He was a homely, smiling dog who wouldn't take "Skat!" for an answer. After a few days he and Viki were romping together, slapping each other playfully, and vocalizing back and forth. One day a little boy came to see her, and the three young animals rolled and wrestled on the lawn. They played tag. They climbed onto lawn chairs and leaped off. While Viki tumbled on the grass, the boy did somersaults, and the dog rolled from side to side on his back. Then Mrs. Clarke's five young cats joined in the fun, a little to one side in the independent way of cats. One of these climbed a tree and Viki was up after it in a flash, while the dog yapped and the boy complained, "Hey, no fair!"

Then all the cats began climbing up and down the tree as Viki tried to catch them. One ran out on a slim branch and Viki could not reach it. Leaning out as far as she dared to go, she pleaded, "Mama! Mama!"

The mother cat was sick, and it did not move from its place in the sun of Mrs. Clarke's back steps. Viki glanced at it now and then and finally she went over to it. The cat did not move. Viki bent over from the waist and looked into its face. Then she kissed it and quietly went away.

Now the manic activity began again, boy, ape, dog, and

cats in a whirlwind of carefree childhood. As I watched I suddenly visualized all of them dressed in clothes and talking together like creatures in a children's story. Perhaps in a minute now they would go walking down the sandy road, a fish pole over each shoulder. It was almost as if species did not exist.

CHAPTER 14.

A Bronx Cheer Pays Off

FOR a few days in May we three put aside our problems and books, and hit the road. We traveled inland to Florida's citrus belt, the Cross Creek country which Marjorie Kinnan Rawlings has portrayed so well. The formal beauty of endless rows of orange trees against rolling hills and the dry sunny air reminded us of California, and we looked our fill. But scenery was wasted on Viki. During the open stretches of landscape she slept or played with her toys in the cool shadow of the dashboard. At first sign of human habitation, however, she was up at the windows, pounding for an audience.

A large part of our trip was spent at orange-juice stands where they challenged us to drink all the juice we could for ten cents. No sooner would we pull into one of these drive-ins than the cry would go up, "It's a monkey!"

In a moment a crowd would materialize from other cars, from houses, and seemingly from sheer space to smile and ask questions. Viki was then in her glory, grinning, waving her monkey doll, and making them shriek with laughter by putting herself through her Imitation Series, clapping her hands, patting her head, poking her fingers into her cheeks, and so on.

Next to the orange-juice stands, our most frequent stops were filling stations. Here, too, we did not go unnoticed. I remember one scene in which we were surrounded by children on their way home from school. There was one little boy trying to get to us from halfway down the block. He was pulling an old lady behind him, and as he came, he cried plaintively, "Hurry, Granny! Oh gosh, can't you hurry! They'll be gone." But we waited for him.

A man stood at the edge of one crowd staring at us for a long time; then he silently went away. Pretty soon he returned with a friend, pointed at Viki, and said, "See?"

On Viki's first night away from home, the manager of the first motel we stopped at took one look at her and hung out his No Vacancy sign. "Species prejudice," Keith muttered.

The second place accepted us, however, and to this day, in all her travels, Viki has never wanted for a night's lodging. She actually leaves these homes-away-from-home cleaner than when she enters, since she amuses herself by polishing the windows with our clothes and sweeping the floor with her somersaulting self.

We spent the next two days at Lake Apopka, where Keith fished and where I sat like a stage prop while Viki entertained the neighbors from a screened porch. Every morning as soon as I unlocked her crib, she hopped out and ran from window to window, peeking out on tiptoes. Sooner or later she found her heart's desire, a row of children squatting in the sand, waiting for her to make an appearance. She waved the contents of our suitcase at them, shoved slices of jelly bread into her face and brushed herself while holding the brush in one foot. After a couple of days I adopted her idea of putting on

Some of Viki's Christmas loot

In interests and abilities she resembled a child at eighteen months

Kitchen helper

Always ready for a ride

a continuous show. I added my bit by running her on her imitation problems.

We were now sure that Viki after four months of training could at last "do this" in imitation of our actions. During this trip she proved very adept at distinguishing between even the most confusingly similar items of the Imitation Series, such as putting a finger in her mouth versus putting one finger into each cheek.

Continuing our trip, we drove through more orange groves, through the Ocala Forest, and finally we stretched our legs by visiting a small zoo near Ocala. Glad to be released after the restraint of motoring, Viki threw herself upon the cool grass, bounded and whirled like a ballet dancer, and smiled ecstatically as the breeze ruffled her sideburns. The customers all left the exhibits to watch this more lively specimen. She rewarded them by doing handstands in which she clicked her heels in mid-air.

Later, as we walked around looking at the caged monkeys, bears, and alligators, Viki grew bored. She hung over my shoulder, held out her hands, and called "Mama!" to the other sightseers.

One day we dropped in on an acquaintance who draws comic strips (in one of which there shortly appeared a fully dressed, shod, and delightfully mischievous baby chimpanzee). Viki swung from the blinds with the people's blessing, bounced on their furniture, and marveled at her hands under a glass-topped table. She seemed to be as aware as we were of the unusual loveliness of the house, but gave one of her rare fear reactions to the exotic bathroom. It was tiled in dark wine with a mirror along one wall where, according to Keith, twenty men could have lined up and shaved simultaneously. It was the dark wine "potty" which elicited Viki's "oo oo, oo oo."

As we returned home to Orange Park, we told each other

that our jaunt had been a complete success, and should some
future event necessitate a longer trip, Viki would make a
fine traveling companion. We were so pleased with Viki's
reaction to the public and their kind interest in her that we
became less hesitant about taking her out. I occasionally took
her shopping with me now and she always accompanied us
to the drive-in theater which had recently opened near our
house. This was the Hayes family's idea of a big night out—
to bundle the baby into her sleepers, polish up the windshield,
and head for the movies.

Viki always watched the first item on the program intently
since this was a color cartoon, but after that she entertained
herself by peering into the adjacent cars. The people peered
back and a good time was had by all, excepting perhaps those
parents whose little children pointed at Viki and wailed, "I
want one!"

So many strangers referred to Viki as "he" that vanity
compelled me to make a drastic change in her attire. The next
time her supply of T-shirts ran low, I bought her a pretty
white dress, printed with tiny rosebuds. When Keith saw it
he clapped a hand to his forehead and stared incredulously;
but Viki was definitely pleased. She held very still as I slipped
it over her head and then she sat smoothing the skirt out
around her. The first time she climbed a door jamb in her dress
and leaped down, the skirt flew up into her face. She grinned
and tried it again and again.

The rear of her skirt poked up in an intriguing way as she
ran about the house on all fours, but she kept tripping over
the hem in front until she devised a simple precaution. She
began holding the front of her dress in her mouth as she ran.

Her first dress did not make her any more feminine, but
it did cause people to treat her more gently, and this mood

was quickly transmitted to the suggestive Viki. For the first time she exhibited pride of ownership; she saw her dress through the laundering process with a very proprietary interest, sometimes taking it from the washline and carrying it into the trees with her.

Viki had only recently come into her arboreal birthright, though the full skirt sailing about her in the breeze made her a fairly atypical chimpanzee. Mrs. Clarke was delighted at seeing Viki overhead in her pecan trees. A frequent scene at this time was Mrs. Clarke reaching up to catch the little ape, who sat in the crook of the tree just out of reach.

I dreaded the day when we must leave our pleasant home in the Pecan Grove, but the need for larger quarters was becoming increasingly urgent. Viki grew daily bigger and stronger, a more proficient climber, and with her new interest in imitation, she was into everything. For twelve hours a day I must watch her and guard our possessions. The tensions were mounting in our little house.

No one realized how badly she needed a room of her own more than Viki herself. When we were forced to stay indoors on rainy days she was very inhibited. Our bedroom was taboo, the kitchen was fragile, and in the living room sat her mama who chanted "No! No!" with the regularity of a metronome. She finally appropriated the front hall and the Blums' stairway for a play space. To get into the house people had to step high over her assortment of blocks and stuffed animals. There was no longer any doubt that both Viki and her folks would be happier in a bigger house.

The possibility of a solution appeared in the fact that the Blums were thinking of buying a home of their own. Mrs. Clarke assured us that if they should find a suitable place before we did, we could rent the entire house and rearrange it to suit our needs. Anything which kept Viki in the Pecan Grove would be acceptable to her, she said, and so the matter rested for the time being.

Outdoors Viki's life was still free and happy in the trees, her swing, and most recently, her wading pool. We were introducing Viki to water play gradually in the hope that we might eventually answer the question: Can apes swim?

For two months Viki had resisted all attempts to get her into the small canvas pool. She dipped her hands, an elbow, a foot, or even the top of her head in the water; she played endlessly at trying to sink her toy boats, but she herself would not be submerged. Finally one summer day I filled the pool with warm soapy water and bathed her in it. After that she splashed merrily through the long hot summer. Now we began looking for a deeper pool in which to test her native swimming ability or to teach her to swim if necessary.

As Viki approached two years of age the Imitation Series paid off by giving her a second word. It had started as a play sound very like a human's Bronx cheer. It was a repulsive sound to us, but we were determined not to discourage any vocal play. Since the original purpose of the Imitation Series had been as an aid in speech training, we had added the cheer to her "do this" repertoire when she was twenty months old. Two months later we began insisting on softer and shorter "p's" with relaxed lips. Finally at twenty-three months, we called for just two "p's" in succession. The result was a whispered but perfectly audible "papa." She immediately used "mama" and "papa" interchangeably in asking for food or favors, since she had no idea what either word meant as yet.

Although we had now proved to our own satisfaction that imitation can be a useful pedagogical tool, we soon learned that it can also be a headache. Viki and I had been playing for some time with a key and padlock, and I had taught her to turn the key in imitation. It did not occur to us at the time that our brand-new car, a Plymouth, is started by simply turning the ignition key to the extreme right. I was washing the car one day, having first parked in reverse as usual and having put Viki inside of it to keep her from getting wet and dirty. I was polishing a door when suddenly I heard the motor begin turning over. Then to my horror the car lurched backward! It was headed straight for the fishpond!

I threw the door open and dived in head first to press the brake pedal with my hand. Luckily the motor stalled. We were shaky but safe. Viki clung to me crying "Oo oo, oo oo."

Thus we learned to beware of a chimpanzee's powers of generalization. By teaching her to use one key we had unwittingly taught her to use all keys. And to think that we had considered having her strike a match as an imitation problem!

If we can expect to be a little sorry for everything that Viki learns, so that in every good there is some evil, by the same token some of Viki's most unpleasant experiences turn out to be her most valuable lessons. For instance, Viki had always chased the harmless snakes in which Florida abounds. I had worried a great deal that she would corner a poisonous snake. Then one morning as we ran out onto the dewy lawn, we almost stepped on a four-foot rattler. I snatched Viki by the skirt, and summoning all my strength, hurled her far behind me. She lay on the grass screaming while the snake slowly moved away. But before it did, it lashed out toward me just once, its eyes cold and brilliant. The encounter left me nauseated all day, and Viki was very quiet and clingy. While this was an unpleasant adventure, it seems to have taught Viki to avoid serpents. A week later, as we were going into the house, I saw my second coral snake. Viki saw it, too, and she clutched the hem of my skirt. We stood perfectly still until the snake had slithered under the house. Neither on this occasion nor ever since has Viki challenged any sort of snake.

Our summer came to an end in a whiz-bang montage of crises. Ruth left town, and the new girl while very pretty and dainty was too gentle to endure for long in our house. After a couple of weeks with Viki she decided to go back to school.

Viki bumped into my face with her hard little head, giving me a black eye and breaking my glasses. Since this was the third such occurrence within a year, I reconciled myself to horn-rimmed chimp-proof affairs.

Three of Viki's young friends went home and broke out with measles. For ten days we anxiously waited to see if she would also have the disease. But she did not, supporting the opinion of the experts that the anthropoid apes do not catch the "childhood diseases" of man.

Finally we huddled over a candle for five days while the edges of a hurricane battered at the house, cutting off our electric power and hemming us in. When the storm passed away, the summer went with it, but our greatest crisis loomed ahead. Soon Keith would go to Denver for the national convention of the American Psychological Association, leaving us girls at home on our own untested resources.

CHAPTER 15.

Apes Is Apes and Cats Is Cats

WHEN Keith left for Denver on the first of September, I was none too enthusiastic about spending two weeks alone with Viki. To my relief and delight, however, Keith's folks decided at this time to pay us a visit. They had been anxious to see Viki ever since Grandma's report to the family. In fact they were so interested in her that I regularly sent them carbons of the diary entries.

In the days which elapsed between Keith's departure and their arrival, the latest maid and I cleaned house furiously. Willye was an intelligent young woman who was accustomed to living with young children. Viki, of course, immediately began testing her resistance. She nipped the girl's legs and was slapped emphatically. She ran off with the dish rag and Willye calmly reclaimed it. Willye adopted my technique for getting Viki down when the little ape carried laundry high into the trees. She came into the house and slammed the door. When Viki realized that she was alone outside, she came screaming out of the trees. The stolen garments remained aloft, however, and when winter turned the pecan

111

trees into gray etchings, our missing socks and undies could be seen flapping against the sky, mute testimony to our daughter's greatest skill.

Early on a Sunday morning, Viki and I drove to the depot to pick up the folks. Mom, short and round and jolly, scooped us into her arms, saying, "Oh, when I saw that dear little face, I could have cried," and she did a little.

Pa looked on smiling shyly, a handsome older version of Viki's "papa." All the way home Mom begged Viki for a kiss while Pa lectured on not rushing this thing. "Let her come to you of her own accord," he said.

Viki remained standoffish throughout the prolonged brunch, during which the folks and I became reacquainted. Although they had read about Viki's schoolwork, this did not compare with the marvel of *seeing* her eat with a spoon. And when she left the table to play with the hurdy-gurdy which they had sent her, their admiration knew no bounds.

All afternoon Pa watched her from a distance while Mom tried every trick to get Viki into her arms. The little one did join her in a brief dance, but when Mom swooped down for a hug, Viki escaped to the top of the refrigerator. Mom held up her arms beseechingly, but Viki only backed away, chuckling. Next Mom experimented at giving Viki commands. She beamed with pleasure when Viki obeyed her first "No! No!"

As I was preparing supper, I heard Mom say, "Go to the bathroom!" and then "Lie down on the diaper board!"

I hurried in, saying, "Oh, she won't let you do that. She never lets strangers—"

But by the time I reached the bathroom, Mom, not knowing it was impossible, had succeeded in changing Viki's diapers. For the remainder of their visit she made this one of her chores. She had brought Viki a pair of pink silk panties with blue ribbons and lace, but alas, her gift was still premature, although Viki had just turned two years of age.

Unimpressed by Mom's rapid progress, Pa was still holding off. "Don't throw yourself at her," he cautioned. "Let her come to you."

Viki finally "came to him" that evening. He had brought with him several pieces of silver jewelry which he makes as a hobby. As he showed these to me along with some of the tools he uses, Viki edged in for a closer look. He chased her away. She sassed him back by stamping her foot and hooting. Mom laughed gaily, but Pa raised his eyebrows and took a second look at our "baby." When we turned in for the night— with me on the living-room couch and them in the bedroom— Pa glanced at Viki's locked crib in the corner and said, "She can't get out of there, can she?"

Seeing the visitors still here on Monday morning, Viki began at once to establish the dominance hierarchy. As if Mom's boldness had taken her by surprise, Viki now began biting at these strange hands which dared to touch her diaper pins. Mom took my advice after a few incidents and slapped her soundly. Soon she and Viki understood each other perfectly.

Pa's hard-to-get attitude was a challenge, and at the first opportunity, Viki "got" him. She sank her teeth into his paunch, leaving a bruise which Pa used as evidence during the rest of his visit.

She also raided their possessions. She clopped about the house in Mom's high heels looking like Minnie Mouse. Once we found her perched atop their open suitcase, Pa's hat on her head and his belt around her middle as she solemnly worked at the new principle of a buckle.

The folks brought to our house the concept of the *Kaffee-klatsch*, which is almost a tribal rite in their native Milwaukee.

It resembles the Englishman's tea except that it features coffee and may take place at any time of the day or night, preferably in the kitchen. However, our folks also love picnics, so that all their food, be it a simple cup of coffee or a full-course dinner, must be carried outdoors for consumption.

Viki followed the trays of food with eager barks and ate her share on the run, climbing over and under the picnickers. When she had finished she was off for a swing through the trees, followed by a splash in the pool. Emerging from the water she would dig in the sand until filthy and then leap into the pool again. Now back to the food trays again, wet and sandy, to be met by a chorus of protest. At that she would dive over the trays and back into the trees. Pa shook his head in mute disapproval of this sort of thing.

However, the worst crime that Viki ever committed in his estimation was probably not sprinkling sand in his coffee, or even biting his paunch. He is extremely fond of cats, and Viki is only fond of chasing them. Mrs. Clarke's collection, attracted by our first picnic-*Kaffeeklatsch*, began wandering over. Pa watched their approach with "aw" written all over his face. But just as he tenderly reached down to caress them, Viki bristled and put on a Gargantuan show of strength. The cats turned as one and went streaking over the lawn. For that I think Pa never forgave her.

Tuesday was a hard day for Viki. The house teemed with guests, since two more people had arrived unexpectedly. Willye of the methodical mind was trying once again to organize our too abundant goods into our too few storage spaces. I was rushing about, officiating at *Kaffeeklatsches* and trying to keep Viki from annoying Pa, who was out under the trees making jewelry.

In the afternoon Henry Nissen escorted us on a tour of the

Laboratory. The folks were fascinated by the big apes, but Viki as usual did not even glance at them. Then we came to the large enclosure which houses six young apes, aged three to five. These little fellows are not timid like the nursery babies and they became very excited about my furry little girl with the big ears and the pink dress. Viki who had been nervous all day clutched me more tightly. Now suddenly, as the youngsters tried to touch her through the wire, she became very frightened. She began whimpering softly. She held me close, and for good measure reached out and pulled Mom's arm around her too. Not until we were home safely established over a cup of coffee did Viki stop shivering. In a vague disturbing way, this incident puzzled me. It was so unlike Viki to be afraid.

On Tuesday evening we were planning to have a picnic as usual, but this one was to include Mrs. Clarke and Henry Nissen, as well as our latest guests. While Mom and I bustled about in the kitchen, Pa sat watching us from the big chair in the living room. Mom had told him to keep Viki out of our way. Nevertheless, the little monkey was all over the kitchen. She tasted food. She wrote on the window with a dill pickle. And she kept sailing through the air in mighty leaps from the refrigerator to the top of the swinging door, narrowly missing the dish cupboard on each trip.

Then, preoccupied with last-minute fixings, one of us cooks carelessly left the cupboard door open. The stage was set. Viki took off from the door, headed for the refrigerator. Instead, she made an unscheduled landing atop the ill-balanced cupboard door. There was an ominous swish of sliding dishes, a thunderous crash, a scream and then—utter chaos!

Mom stood marooned at the stove, hemmed in by a pile of broken dishes a foot high and three feet across, a pile from

which rose the fumes of a broken bottle of gin. Viki perched
on the refrigerator, very worried and frightened but un-
injured. I packed her off to her crib, the one place where I
knew she would be safe from broken glass. My next thought
was of the anticipated guests. I tossed Mom a broom and
told her to dig her way out.

When Henry arrived, we were sweeping fragments of china
and glass and splashes of gin under the sink and into the
pantry, out of sight. "Pay no attention to this," I was saying
hysterically. "The people will want to eat. Pay no attention
to this."

"I thought you were going to watch her," Mom scolded Pa.

"I *was* watching her," he insisted. "I sat right here and
saw the whole thing."

Luckily we still had dishes enough for roughing it since we
had already set the picnic table. Leaving the mess behind,
we took Viki and went out into the peaceful open air. Later
the folks and I cleaned the kitchen. We found only three
useable pieces, which we saved as a surprise for Willye, who
was already complaining about our cluttered cupboards. We
greeted her the next morning saying, "We cleaned out the
dish cupboard for you, Willye."

She opened it to find a small vase on the clean top shelf,
a ten c.c. graduate on the clean middle shelf, and on the
bottom shelf, a teapot without a handle. To our disappoint-
ment she scarcely batted an eyelash. Perhaps she had been
in the Hayes house long enough to expect this sort of thing;
or she may have heard the crash at her home, half a mile
down the road.

One day, after the folks had been here for a week, I decided to run Viki through all her current problems, as entertainment for them and a review for her. While I was as-

sembling the equipment we lost half of our audience. Pa
went over to play with the cats, warning us to keep Viki here
at home; but Mom saw a fair sample of Viki's accomplishments at two years.

We presented a string of imitations very rapidly and without
error, including many which required close attention and
discrimination. I pointed out to Mom that blowing a whistle
when the teacher does so is no real test of imitation if this
is the only task which can be done with a whistle. I showed
her how Viki could duplicate my actions when I either blew
the whistle, pounded with it, "scribbled" with it, or slipped
the end of it over my finger.

I also devised an impromptu imitation problem using the
toy cash register which the folks had given Viki for her second
birthday. Saying, "Do this!" I would press down a key. When
the drawer flew open, I would put a raisin inside and close
it. Viki then pressed the same key, the drawer again opened,
and she claimed the raisin. A variation required Viki to open
the drawer, take out a toy coin, and "buy" a raisin from me.

We also demonstrated traditional chimpanzee problems
such as the one in which Viki moved a chair to reach a suspended toy. In another problem, Viki had been getting raisins
for the past three months by joining a pair of sticks, either
of which was too short by itself to reach the raisin. But today she seemed utterly unable to put the small stick into the
hole of the larger one. Investigating the apparatus, I found
that a mud dauber wasp had built its nest in the hole! After
that Mom never questioned my extravagant tales of insect
life in Florida.

Later in the day Mom and Viki sat under the trees, in-
dustriously at work on their sewing. They made a charming
if unorthodox family portrait. Mom's stitches were neat and
prim, while Viki threaded her huge darning needle with ribbon

and flamboyantly plunged it in and out of a mesh orange sack until she ended up with a tangled wad of ribbon and mesh.

That night we went to the drive-in movie theater. Pa was reluctant to let me drive at night with Viki on my lap, but I insisted that she would be completely reliable. She sat facing me, hugging me around the waist, not once touching the wheel. At the show, she straddled the open window, munching popcorn, and admiring Woody the Woodpecker. When this best part was over, she snuggled sleepily into my lap. Mom said, "Isn't she sweet!" And just at this point, Viki bit a hole in my paper cup of grape soda water.

One day Mrs. Clarke drove us to St. Augustine, the oldest city in the United States. While the others went sightseeing Viki and I waited in the car and answered the questions of passersby. That day Viki required diaper changes at the oldest house, the oldest fort, and the oldest schoolhouse in America, and also at the Fountain of Youth.

During the last days before Keith's return, Mom and I spent hours looking at maps, since she and I were planning to drive to the Smokies as soon as Keith got home to take care of Viki. Pa would return to Milwaukee by himself. He seldom took part in our activities during those last days. He had had his jewelry-making equipment upset once too often by the gay and leaping chimpanzee.

One afternoon he did join us in the yard for a *Kaffeeklatsch*. Viki took a sip of Mom's coffee, and a sip from mine, but when she approached Pa's he shooed her away. She resented this and nipped at his feet. When I slapped her, she climbed a low branch and sailed to and fro, just missing Pa's head on each swing. Finally he took a deep breath and said what had perhaps been on his mind for days: "What I'd like to know is how long you intend to go on with this thing?"

I answered that if he meant the experiment, it was expected to run indefinitely. "The number of questions we might be able to answer with a unique specimen like this grows greater for every day she spends in the human environment."

"You should *see* some of the things she can do!" Mom slipped in.

"Also, we feel responsible for her future," I continued. "And we have grown very fond of her."

"Of course, you have!" Mom said, "And she *is* a cute little thing."

Pa raised his eyes to the heavens. And then he ducked quickly as Viki came flying out of the tree. "Sure she's cute," he cried, "if you can stand it. But you can't expect people to come to your house if she bites them, jumps all over them, keeps them on the run—"

I hastened to apologize for her recent behavior. There was no denying that Viki had given Pa a rough time. It worried me. Viki did not seem to be herself lately. She was more wild, less obedient, given to more frequent tantrums and strange fears.

But now Pa was off on a new tack. "Let's be practical for a moment," he said, fixing a shrewd businessman's eye on me. "How many cupboards full of dishes can you afford to buy? Where is your financial future in this business?"

"People don't become research scientists to make money, Pa, and Keith wouldn't be happy doing anything else." After that the conversation bogged down, and in a while Pa trudged over the lawn to Mrs. Clarke's. There he sat on a bench in the sunshine, stroking a kitten. In a few days Keith would be home. Perhaps then Pa would again bring up the subject. He might expect to find more sense in a man, a male of his own flesh and blood. But I feared that he would receive only the same unsatisfying answers.

CHAPTER 16.

The Lapse

LEAVING Keith and Viki with a good supply of food and diapers, and not enough dishes to make a dirty sinkful, Mom and I headed for the Smokies. We had a wonderful binge, five days of unruffled, unmauled calm. But then a terrible homesickness seized me. Since Mom decided that she was just as lonesome for Pa, I put her on a bus for Milwaukee and turned my car south.

Sixteen hours later, in the middle of the night, I crossed the cattle guard into the Pecan Grove.

I awoke the next morning with the well-known sense of unreality which comes to the returned traveler. I could not quite recognize the quiet darkened bedroom or the faint thuds and "No! No!'s" of my family in the next room. In a little while the door opened and a pretty monkey face fringed in black sideburns peeked around the corner. Very stealthily a small chimpanzee crept into the room, climbed to the foot of the bed, and sat there staring at me. She was a beautiful specimen with thick glossy hair and clear expressive eyes. I assumed that it was Viki, yet in a flash of panic, I realized that I did not remember her at all!

She leaped to the dresser and swung out into space by a drapery cord. Her movements were gracefully monkeylike and seemed incongruous in a house. Now my visitor swung back to the dresser and switched on the lamp. This little act, performed by an ape's hand, also struck me as unreal and yet as strangely familiar.

Next she opened a perfume bottle, sniffed it, and screwed back the cap. She then flicked at her sideburns with a comb. She drew a hairbrush along her furry arm. She picked up a glove and plunged her hand into it. I had seen many good-looking apes in my life, many gymnastic apes, but I had seen only one baby ape going through these manipulations. After that the room rapidly settled into a familiar pattern. When Keith came in a second later to look for his wandering chimpanzee, Viki and I were holding each other close.

Then came my second surprise. Her hairy body, her big ears and eyebrow ridges seemed like some elaborate farce. I knew that this was my baby by her response to me, by the things she did with her hands; but someone had dressed my baby in a monkey costume. Several days elapsed before there was no more embarrassment between us. In that time I was constantly experiencing moments of shock over her athletic contortions and her furriness.

While Keith and I talked about my trip, Viki swung from the blinds, bounded up and down on the couch, and climbed to the top of the back door, where she lay gazing down at us. Nearby on a high shelf, out of her reach before now, stood our electric clock. Viki now demonstrated her latest skill: straddling the top of the door, she shoved off from one wall, making the door swing in an arc. As she came alongside the clock, Viki reached out and daintily flipped it off its shelf.

This sort of activity continued until noon, when a new crisis arose in the kitchen. The only space available for the bread box was on top of the refrigerator, which was also unfortunately the favorite meeting place of our household ants. Keith had ingeniously solved the problem by setting the bread box on a can which was circled with Scotch tape, sticky side out. On top of the box were now placed boxes of cookies, crackers, candy, cereals, up and up and up in a wonderful, ant-free tower. For six months Viki had avoided tipping this over, but accidents will happen. There was a crash, of course, and then I knew for sure that I was home.

Back in my old groove, complete with broom, I swept up soda crackers, gum drops, puffed rice, and pumpernickel. Keith remarked on what was no longer news: "This young girl needs a room of her own. Not a cage, but a place to play when we are not giving her our undivided attention."

This remark had become a cliché in our house, but this time it was not merely wishful talk. The upstairs apartment had been vacated while he was in Denver, and Mrs. Clarke had agreed to rent us the whole house. We began at once to rearrange our enlarged quarters. We decided to make the upstairs taboo to Viki, using that bedroom for ourselves and the upstairs living room as a company parlor. Up the stairs went all our clothes, books, cameras, guns, anything that was not chimpanzee-proof. The downstairs bedroom would be hers, for sleeping and free play. We would continue to use the same kitchen and bath with the downstairs living room serving for normal family use. This left the upstairs kitchen, bathroom, and dining room, which we arranged as a small apartment to be rented out later.

I became convinced that there was something wrong with Viki during this transitional period. As we toted furniture and belongings to and fro, she failed to take it in her merry stride.

She tugged at my skirt, begging to be carried. When I picked her up, she clung to me, and if I sympathized with her, she whimpered and kissed me. Since I was very busy and worn out from the stresses of the summer, I sometimes rejected her pleas for cuddling. She would then clutch her pillow and cry "Oo oo oo." Soon she was spending most of every day sitting listlessly, uninterested in even her favorite games.

My first thought was that she might be physically ill, but there were no symptoms except this alternating anxiety and apathy.

We had expected Viki to be delighted with a room of her own, where all her toys were gathered in one impressive collection, and where no one ever said, "No! No!" However, when the first occasion arose to put her in there with the door closed, she screamed herself breathless. We were no better off for all our moving. Her room was used only for sleeping, and even then we had to wait until she was sound asleep—sometimes midnight—to put her to bed.

At daybreak she was again wide awake. We had not bothered to put blinds on her room since we knew that she would only destroy them, and we had taken the top off her bed in the hope that she would learn to keep herself covered; therefore the first light of day awakened her. Finding herself alone, she would let out such loud terrified screams that we would fall out of bed and be halfway down the stairs before we woke up.

Now her strange recent behavior took a new twist. Where before she had clung to me crying like a baby, she now rejected me with set lips and cold eyes. She began running away for the first time in her life. If I called her back, she climbed a tree. The trick of coming into the house without her no longer worked. She ran wild in the Pecan Grove, breaking some of Mrs. Clarke's best plants. When I finally decided to keep her locked in the house, she broke a window and sailed right through the screen.

Worst of all, her pleasant personality had disappeared. Once, after I had spanked her for biting Willye, she faced me with angry barks. This in turn made me very angry. We would just see if she could dominate me! Taking the stick which had brought her out of a disobedient streak a year before, I spanked her as hard as I could. She did not cry or move a muscle until I threw the stick aside and burst into tears. She then picked up the stick, and holding one end in each hand, she cracked it in two with her foot. Previously she had rushed to comfort anyone who shed even mock tears. Now she simply stared at me with pouted lips.

I knew then that something terrible was happening to us.

The evidence was all around us in broken windows, demolished toys, and torn clothing, for if she was forced to stay in her room, she ripped her clothes and diapers to shreds. In addition to her morning reveille she began screaming in the middle of the night. I resented this and she drew farther and farther away from my resentment.

Her biting became common gossip. Our friends solicitously sent us cartoons, one of which portrayed a baby crawling under a park bench while an old gentleman complained to its nursemaid, "Well by gad, Madam, *something* nipped me!"

Viki's toilet training became worse than ever. She stopped smiling completely. She refused to eat, she refused to play, she forgot how to say her words. Seemingly overnight all her "schoolwork" disintegrated. All day long and far into the night, she simply ran around with a wild look in her eyes.

Now suddenly, I became really frightened. Was this the end of our experiment? How could we go on like this; yet how could I bear to put Viki in a cage? What had happened to disturb her, not in one, but in all areas—personality, play, social behavior, and schoolwork? What could possibly turn an intelligent agreeable little creature into a perfect monster, all in the brief space of a month?

As I looked squarely at our lives, I saw more than sufficient cause. All summer long our house had overflowed with people and excitement. We had each gone off on trips, upsetting her routine. We had disrupted her home by moving things around, arriving at a plan which was in no way suitable to her needs, a plan which had even disturbed her sleeping schedule.

As I looked back, I could see many foreshadowings of our present trouble. During the folks' visit there had been her fear of the Laboratory apes, her harassing of Pa, her abnormal spells of clinging in terror. Some friends had said it was "the chimp in her coming out." But any child, subjected to the same neglect and insecurity, might be expected to react in the same way—first seeking comfort in its mother, and finding no comfort, rejecting its training and withdrawing into itself. We had been referring to this bad spell as her "lapse." Now I realized that it was our lapse, not hers.

How were we to make Viki happy again?

We decided that first of all the house must be made more adequate to the needs of our experiment. Keith removed the solid wooden door from her room and replaced it with a heavy screen door through which she could watch the household activity and see why she was being temporarily confined. We put the top back on her bed, making it the cosy light-tight nest to which she had become accustomed. Keith made plans to cover the insides of the windows with stout screening to avoid further breakage.

By thus providing optimal housing, we hoped to minimize the necessity of inhibiting Viki too greatly. For we realized that discipline could be carried just so far. A chimpanzee can take more punishment than any decent person should be willing to give. And because of her verbal deficit she could not be reached by bribes, or threats of lost favors, as children traditionally are. How could Santa Claus be held over the head of a chimpanzee? No, our only choice was to give our subject a home which was tough enough to contain her and so pleasant that future mental upsets would not occur.

While Keith fitted our house to the needs of our work, I devoted all my time to winning Viki back. She had been refusing her bath vehemently, but when I added a salt to the water which produced fascinating bubbles, she climbed into the tub to investigate. I sat nearby, but did not try to handle her. After she had splashed for an hour in the warm soapy water, I invited her to come and be dried. She stared at me without interest. I got out our best bath towel, a fluffy rose one which Viki had never seen. She was too curious to resist. She nuzzled her face into it a little, and then let me pat her dry. I tickled her a little. She squirmed away, but before she did, I was rewarded with her first grin in weeks. I did not try to dress her, nor did I feed her. I simply set dishes of interesting food upon the table and called her attention to them. She helped herself. That night as she was falling asleep on the couch, she stiffened suspiciously when I stroked her sideburns, but she did not move away.

The next day I put an assortment of her blocks on the table, and began building towers by myself. She came to watch. Then she climbed up and built a tower also. On an off chance that she might be able to match forms, I held up a red cube, saying, "Do you have one like this?"

No interest. I tapped a red cube near her and held up the two together. Next I held out a yellow cylinder. "Do you have one like this?" I asked again, and then pointed to another yellow cylinder.

Taking it very slowly I introduced the new game. To my surprise, she quickly realized what I wanted and seemed to exhibit a certain pride of accomplishment as she confidently held out each block to match mine.

Then I moved this game, and as many other activities as possible, to her room to make it seem like a desirable place. After the door was completed, however, she seldom objected to going to her room, even if no one was with her.

I bought her a pretty new wardrobe of yellow T-shirts and a gray corduroy jumper. She seemed to like these, and stopped tearing her clothes deliberately—unless she had good cause to feel neglected. (To this day if she has been confined in her room too long, she invariably tears her clothes in protest.)

We had to retrain her to say "mama" from the very beginning. We asked her to say "ahhh," and then shaped the mouth for the m. But she only took one day to relearn it, and "papa" came along with it. Not only that, but she was suddenly able to do all the various problems she had been able to do before the lapse.

Her sensational recovery convinced us that our diagnosis had been correct. But the fact that her biting had become rare, that she slept the night through, ate like someone making up for lost weight, and obeyed our commands, were extra blessings. For me it was enough that Viki smiled again. As suddenly as she had gone away, the old Viki returned, and with her a rapport between us such as is usually reserved for Siamese twins.

CHAPTER 17.

A Cup of Good Cheer

THE final step in the reorganization of our household was renting the small upstairs apartment. When the real-estate gentleman arrived with our prospective tenants, I was busy in the kitchen. I called to him to take the Lawtons up and said that I would follow shortly. A few seconds later I noticed that Viki was not with me and that the front door was open. At that exact moment, a shrill scream of terror came from upstairs.

I dashed up to find Mrs. Lawton staring aghast at Viki, who was stamping her foot and hooting in triumph at the reaction she had produced. Mrs. Lawton explained that she had been examining the closet, and had not witnessed the entrance of what the real-estate gentleman described as "a little baby monkey." She had turned to the kitchen, and there, grinning at her from atop the refrigerator, was Viki, looking considerably larger from that angle.

In spite of this upsetting introduction, the Lawtons moved in, and rapidly became good friends with Viki. All work must stop as she watched them come and go, and after a few weeks, she began trotting bowleggedly up the stairs to visit them.

Although Viki's schoolwork and personality had quickly returned to normal after our lapse, she continued to run away occasionally—not to escape from us, but rather to call on her friends, the Lawtons, or her old pal Mrs. Clarke. If the landlady was not in sight when Viki wanted to go over there, she took my hand and led me along with her. The big attraction at this time of year was a small tree heavy with golden tangerines. If I let her pluck just one, she was content to be carried home, peeling her prize on the way.

Our preparations for Christmas proceeded tranquilly and without incident. When Viki was in a calm co-operative mood, I invited her to help me, but if she was manic when I had work to do, I said quietly, "Go to your room." And she obeyed without complaint. I rarely left her there alone for more than thirty minutes, but if I did, she came to the screen door and called "Mama!"

I could bribe her to wait for a few more minutes by slipping a Christmas cookie under the door. She quickly caught on to this trick; now when she wanted out, she pushed toy money from her cash register under the door at me.

She liked her room so well on the whole that if her play in the living room was inhibited by too many "No! No!'s," she ran into her room of her own accord, hooting at us indignantly over her shoulder.

Two of the devices we had introduced to help Viki over the lapse now gave us handsome results. We had originally allowed her to play in bathtubs full of warm soapy water as a play therapy. It seemed to calm her and make her feel comfortable and secure. We did not hope in this way to add evidence to the question of whether or not she could swim or learn to swim. In fact, we had set aside that problem for the winter months.

Now, during her bath, Viki began paddling her hands in the water. Then she hung onto the edge of the tub and kicked with her feet. When I held her under the tummy, as children are held for swimming lessons, she made the proper motions. I then took my hands away, and to my amazement, she remained completely suspended for five seconds before her feet sought bottom. She seemed delighted. Although she coughed and sputtered from the water in her nose, she always laughed and went back for more.

Once again we almost had cause to regret her latest achievement. She became so fond of water that one wintry day, she ran away to Mrs. Clarke's and jumped into the ice-cold fishpond. However, I rushed her home for dry clothes and no harm came of it.

Toward the end of the lapse I had introduced a new game in which she gave me a block to match the one I held up. Now we combined this with tower-building. From my set of assorted blocks, I would select a yellow cube, for example. Viki then took a yellow cube from her set of blocks. I next placed a red cylinder atop my yellow cube. Viki did likewise. Then a blue wheel, a long orange cylinder, a Tinker Toy wheel, and so on, up and up and up in two identical towers. She was, of course, enjoying it as a game, but it was valuable training as well. Perhaps later she would copy my *finished* tower, or even a picture of one.

It is said that a father seldom finds real companionship in his child until it reaches the responsive age of two years. At about that time Keith and Viki also began to enjoy each other more. Some days I felt like the third man in a crowd of three. When he came home at night, she greeted him with excited pleasure barks and general manhandling. In fact, she started sounding her greeting as soon as his car appeared out on the highway. This puzzled us, since a neighbor in the Grove, who came home every evening at about the same time as Papa, was never hailed, although he also drove a new green Plymouth exactly like ours. She could not possibly have discriminated between the two men as far away as the highway. We finally noticed that there *was* one small difference between the cars which may have been her cue. The neighbor's car had gleaming, white sidewall tires!

One of the many games at which Keith and Viki spent their evenings involved her little brown stuffed dog. Keith would say, "Bring me your dog!" and Viki would run off to find it. When she returned to him with the dog, she was very insistent about his taking it. If he teased her by holding his hands in his pockets, or behind him, she tugged and tugged until she pulled out the hidden hand. Then she slapped the dog into it emphatically, and galloped away. It was then his obligation to toss it into the air for her to catch, or else scoot it across the floor so that it "chased" her.

In a variation of the dog game, Keith tossed it across the room into an orange crate. Viki's job was to dig it out and return it to him for another toss. She was at an age when children are very conservative about following the rules of a game. When Keith tossed the dog once and missed the box, Viki picked it up, put it into the box, and took it out again before returning it to him. He made a point of missing occasionally after that, and she continued to "fix it" for him, but soon reduced her efforts to a mere token wave in the direction of the box.

Sometimes now I turned Viki over to Keith for work sessions, while I looked on. Accustomed to my rapid-fire stream of "do this'es," Viki became very impatient with Keith's more deliberate commands. For each individual item he asked her to imitate, she ran through her entire repertoire, patting her head, clapping her hands, nodding her head, and so on. "Wait now, wait!" Keith would cry. "Just do *this!*" At which Viki would shake her hands from the wrists nervously as if anxious to get on with the session.

When the problem involved a mechanism, I think she valued Keith's demonstrations more than mine. At any rate, besides watching his use of a new tool, she now began asking him to "do it again" by taking his hands, placing them on the object, and then staring intently. If he hesitated, she said "Papa" to him, or sometimes "Mama."

Since the Imitation Series had already proved useful as a language aid by giving Viki her second word, we now added several more sounds and mouth movements to our list of "do this'es." These included a kissing sound, clicking the teeth, sticking out the tongue, "tsk," and "k," which she made by holding her hand over her nose and exhaling with the back of the tongue against the soft palate. We did not teach Viki how to make these sounds; she had previously made them in play as many chimpanzees do. In that respect they are similar to the human child's babbling. However, they are not voiced, but are produced by mouth movements and vibration alone. What we taught her was merely to repeat these sounds back to us when we produced them—which chimpanzees do not ordinarily do.

Since her language deficit involved understanding as well as speaking, we were also coaching her to touch her nose or ear on command, or to give us her hand or her foot when we asked her to. Sometimes she did this excellently; on other days she was completely confused.

As the schools closed for Christmas vacation, Viki had her usual influx of young visitors. A year before some had found her a merry playmate, but this year, while she obviously loved to be near them, she was too rough to play with children less than five years old. Although she weighed only twenty-six pounds and was just twenty-eight months old, her hands and arms were much stronger than theirs. As soon as we saw them tremble before her inevitable bluster, we avoided unpleasant scenes by putting either Viki or the children into her room. They found her toys novel and intriguing, but few youngsters paid her a second call.

A notable exception was a new little girl in town, Chrissie Kleemeier, who is exactly the same age as Viki. There is a fay quality about Chrissie, an enchanted twinkle that suggests she might enjoy a chimpanzee playmate. She is a sensitive child, but not skittish, and being the child of two psychologists, perhaps she was more adequately prepared than most children for meeting Viki. In any case, she was not visibly afraid. She looked at Viki with a characteristic air of breathless reserve, while our little chimpanzee, who reserves nothing, put on a three-ring display of her powers. When Chrissie did not flinch, Viki stared back at her for a few seconds. Then she took the little girl's arms and danced her from side to side. This and walks about the yard were the gist of their early contacts, but Viki was very gentle with her new friend, and I had great hopes for their future.

Viki's most frequent young caller was still Jimmy Tarr. He is that admirable sort of child who is not aggressive but who will not be trod upon either. Being seven years old, he was Viki's equal physically. One day he played with her for almost five hours!

A great part of this time was spent in wrestling and cuffing, with Jimmy periodically reminding Viki that he did not intend to be bitten even if baby chimps *did* do this in play. After an hour of roughhouse they both flopped down to rest, but after they had eaten a peck or so of Christmas cookies, they were ready to go again. They played hide-and-seek, tag, peekaboo. They climbed trees. Jimmy showed Viki the possibilities of Tinker Toys and she demonstrated the use of her Pump-a-Ball.

The usually possessive Viki made the great concession of letting Jimmy play with her monkey dolls. These two dolls were almost as big as Viki herself and they were her constant companions. She pulled them about by their tails so that they made fine pulltoys. She lay on her back and juggled them with her feet. She kissed them until their faces lost form, and holding one on each knee, she sat in the front window, giving passersby an impression of an awful lot of monkeys.

Jimmy wanted Viki to throw the monkeys to him, but while she was good at catching, she could not yet throw either a ball or a ball substitute. Jimmy showed aptitude for becoming an experimental psychologist by this observation: "If you want her to throw the monkeys to you and she won't, you should say 'Do this or you won't get any cookies.' Then I bet she'd do it."

Jimmy's mother said he arrived home completely exhausted. Viki also was too tired to eat her supper. In her sleepers, she ran outside for a last fling through the trees, and then she tumbled wearily into bed.

Viki received our holiday callers with great hospitality. She brought them her dog, she led them into her room, but I'm afraid she also picked their pockets of nickels, dimes, and occasional quarters. Her new interest in money may have been generalized from her cash register, but the Law would probably turn a deaf ear to this perfectly valid explanation.

After Jimmy's visit, our house abounded in Viki's primitive Tinker Toy constructions. Parents reasoned that if Viki could be inspired by Jimmy, then younger children should copy her accomplishments. When I mentioned that Viki had learned to ride her tricycle, one couple asked if they might bring their little girl to watch, since she had not yet mastered the idea of pedaling. They came, but they left in a hurry when they saw Viki's technique. She holds her feet out to the side, leans over the handlebars, and works the pedals with her hands!

The high spot of our Christmas season was a wedding party for a visiting couple. It was our first chance to use the upstairs company parlor, and we made it gay with holly, flowers, candles and a wedding cake which floundered under enormous frosting roses. Viki was very excited about the fancy trimmings. With her hands clutching the backs of her thighs, she walked about the room upright, peering at the little sandwiches, the salted nuts, the tiny candies shaped like flowers, and above all, the beautiful cake. This alone seemed irresistible, and I caught her several times on the very brink of biting into it. She gave herself away actually, for although she approached it in an unconcerned way which did not arouse my suspicions, she could not inhibit her loud food barks, which came bursting out at the very last minute. She was foiled again and again.

On the afternoon of the party, Viki was right at home amidst the smoke and clamor of twenty people. She fingered the party gowns, shook hands with one and all, and kissed a favored few. Since her taste for alcohol had not yet died out, she also bummed sips of cocktails. I did not approve of this practice, and pledged the people not to indulge her. They saw no harm, however, in offering her the cherries from their Manhattans. Since Viki loves cherries, she ate a great many at this party. I suspect that she occasionally had to drain a glass to get at the cherry.

In the bustle of being hostess, I forgot to guard the cake. At her first opportunity, Viki slyly helped herself to the first two bites. Luckily the bride was broad-minded. We turned the nibbled side to the wall, and the newlyweds cut the cake. Viki got a frosting rose for her very own, and down it went to join the oysters, Liederkranz, and herring which had gone before.

When I went downstairs to replenish the food supply, I put Viki in her room in the hope that she might take a little nap. Instead she pressed against the screen door in her party dress, pleading eloquently to be taken back to the people. When I trudged back upstairs, I carried food on one arm and Viki on the other, while she solemnly ate my unprotected corsage.

The party again pointed up Viki's worst problem—vocabulary. She had asked the guests for food and drink by saying "Mama" and "Papa." How were we to give her the idea that I alone was "Mama" and Keith was "Papa" if she must use these words for all needs and toward all people? A few days later I was talking to Henry Nissen about the possibility of using her play sounds to give her more words.

"She has a 'k' sound, which she can repeat after us, and a 'p' as in 'papa.' If we could teach her to string 'k' and 'p' together, we would get a primitive 'cup.' "

Viki had been listening to our conversation, and when she heard us join her two favorite play sounds, she immediately said, "k-p."

"She did it!" Henry exclaimed. "She just *said* cup." He sounded a little indignant as he always does when we underestimate the abilities of any chimpanzee.

Viki's third word immediately became her best. She practiced it by herself, and since her thirst is practically unquenchable, she said "cup" perhaps a hundred times a day. Even at three years it is her most dependable word and it definitely means "I want a drink."

Playmates

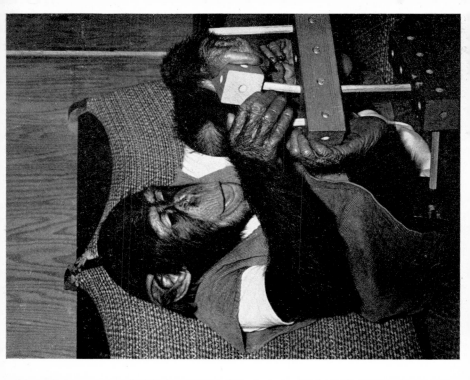

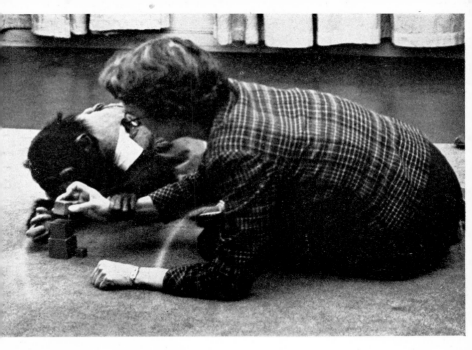

She asked Mrs. Fiedler for another demonstration

Solving the stick and tunnel problem

Looking through her kaleidoscope

Helping with the housework

CHAPTER 18.

We Don't Need Talking Apes

VIKI greeted the New Year by making her first public appearance. On this occasion, we three described and demonstrated our experiment to the Orange Park Women's Club. It is rather unusual for research workers to mount the podium *with* their experimental subject, but so is our work unusual. Any community is made up of homes, and when an ape is being raised in one of these, the community wants to know what is being done, and why. Therefore, when we were asked to tell our town about our ménage, we eagerly accepted the invitation.

Being aware of Viki's abilities as a scene stealer, we decided that I should go to the Clubhouse first to give a little talk, with Keith bringing Viki to the meeting later.

I faced the audience with some trepidation, since more than half of the people were strangers to me. But I took a deep breath and began. First I invited them to come to our house at any time and see our experiment in action. In a part of the world where hospitality is the keynote of social life, this proved to be a fortunate opening. The ladies nodded and smiled as if each were personally acknowledging my invitation.

As I outlined our purposes the ladies listened politely, but not until I began describing life with Viki did anyone lean forward in her chair. They shook their heads sympathetically as I related those of our problems which are common to all parents. But when I told of her aerial gymnastics and her three-dimensional utilization of our house, they glanced at Mrs. Clarke as if for confirmation. She beamed broadly.

I told them of our failures, too, and pointed out that only by studying the shortcomings of lower animals can the true nature of man's superiority be specified.

In conclusion I spoke of Viki's future and assured them that it was in responsible hands; that perhaps we love her a little extra, knowing that she can never live an independent life. At this point three ladies blew their noses.

Now Viki herself arrived in a red corduroy jumper, a flower-embroidered sweater, and an expression of utter innocence. Or perhaps she was only sleepy. In any case, she climbed into my arms and sat very quietly, looking about her. The ladies gathered around to examine the first chimpanzee most of them had ever touched. They listened to her say her words for cookies and coffee. They asked many questions. And over and over again we heard the remark: "I never dreamed what you were doing out there!"

Sometimes this statement was half apologetic and then we knew that we had accomplished our purpose of the evening. We had given these ladies some facts upon which to base their opinions of us and our work. And while we realized that this warm reception was no complete index of public feeling about us, we went home that night surrounded by the comfortable glow of being neighbors to a small town.

We had been planning to publish our findings as soon as possible, but in March a friend beat us to the draw by men-

tioning our work to the press. A little story hit the wire services, and columnists all over the country seemed to consider it
very provocative copy.

The Washington *Star* carried a humorous editorial entitled
"We Don't Need Talking Apes," with the theme that there
is already too much talking in the U.N. without adding a dele-
gation of gorillas. Another columnist suggested that we teach
people to talk intelligently first. Hal Boyle warned that if zoo
apes could talk, they would make ill-natured remarks to the
visitors and complain about the quality of the bananas.

From then on, whenever Keith spoke at a scientific meeting,
or we took a trip with our "talking ape," we could expect to
see our name in print. On the whole the coverage was kind
and frequently amusing, but not nearly so entertaining as the
mail we received afterward.

There were some crank letters, a few words of praise, and
many requests for pictures and story material. Some letters
were coy or secretive, "Get in touch with us. We have news
of special interest to you."

One man offered to write a poem about us "in a jovial manner" for $1.25. Another wanted to put us on television. A third,
who admitted that he knew little about the brain personally,
suggested that if we removed the pineal body from Viki's brain
it might be easier for her to talk.

One clipping told of the census taker who came to our house
and refused Keith's straight-faced request that she tabulate
Viki. With an equally sober face, she said, "They instructed
me about her at the office."

We made a small contribution to the international scene.
An American newspaper man brought out an old cliché:
"What's so unusual about a chimp saying three words? England has been making the American eagle say 'uncle' for
years."

Back from England came: "Talking apes! This must be an example of American know-how."

In general, our reaction to publicity has been to agree with the man who said we don't need talking apes. Nor do we really need talking editorial writers, but both can be entertaining and useful if they are not taken too seriously.

CHAPTER 19.

Great Preparations

THE spring of 1950, which was to climax for us in "The Trip," a month-long whirl of professional travel, began with the three of us under the weather. First Viki caught a heavy cold. She declined all attempts to comfort or amuse her, asking only to be fed canned milk. She was very specific about this. She turned her face away from milk in a cup or *diluted* canned milk. If I would just puncture the can and hand it to her, she required no further catering. She was so independent during this illness that she even learned to blow her nose and use disposable hankies by herself.

No sooner was she well than Keith and I took turns at having a quick but violent virus infection. For the first time, Viki showed real consideration for sick people, perhaps because she herself had been ill so recently. I remember lying on the cot in her room one afternoon, while she played quietly at my feet with Tinker Toys. A car pulled up outside. As our friends habitually do, these unexpected callers came straight to the windows of Viki's room and peeked in. I did not intentionally play possum; it was more a matter of feeling too sick to lift my head. Very carefully, Viki picked her way over my inert form and went to the window. There she greeted the people with her customary hooting, but this time with her lips only. She made no sound and none of her usual pounding. The people said something about "asleep" and drove away. Viki then very slowly and delicately returned to her toys.

As she always does, Viki recovered from her cold all at once, and she was ready for work. She seemed to enjoy the new imitation problem involving duplicate balls of clay. As I pounded my clay ball, poked at it, rolled it on the table, or between my hands, she immediately repeated my actions.

Viki also began setting up problems of her own to work at. One of these was tying a knot. After consulting the child development books, I told her that she probably would not be able to do this for at least two more years; but Viki went right on untying everybody's shoelaces, and trying to retie them. Her procedure was to pull up the two ends, cross them, pause for a bewildered second, and then hurriedly twist the laces round and round each other, finishing with a smart pat, as if to say "There!" She would not accept coaching on this self-imposed problem.

The first human tool which Viki's chimpanzee hands failed to master was the scissors. She could close them for a snip, but then her short thumb was unable to pull them open, so that both hands must be used to open the scissors before she could make the next snip. Six months later she painstakingly cut most of the hair off her tummy in this snip by snip manner, but she still failed the scissors as a test item, since she was unable to hold the scissors in one hand and make a continuous series of cuts.

Her block play showed a new development. Sometimes now, instead of towers, she built horizontally-aligned "trains." This is characteristic, also, of the child approaching three years of age.

Viki began at this time to play with weird structures which she built from Tinker Toys. To Keith these looked like gallows. I based my guess that they were dolls on the fact that she frequently kissed them and covered them with her blanket so that only the tops were showing. We were seeing more and more imaginative play of this sort, but since Viki could not identify it, our policy was simply to record it without unjustified interpretation.

Viki at the age of two-and-one-half was booming—physically, psychologically, and educationally. However her parents were becoming increasingly aware of their own limitations. There were a great many questions about Viki's future which we could not answer. Keith is only one psychologist, whose previous experience has been with other and unrelated problems. I am only an apprentice psychologist and mother, learning both fields as I go along. Our Laboratory friends are ape specialists, but they are not experts in the speech and pre-school education of chimpanzees. If the three of us were to get the most out of this experiment, the time had come to seek expert outside advice. We needed to confer with speech therapists and with teachers skilled in the training of young children, especially abnormal children. We would also like professional testers to evaluate Viki's intelligence.

Gradually the idea of "The Trip" began taking form. Between the middle of April and the middle of May, two psychological meetings would be held in the North and Keith was planning to attend these. If he drove, taking Viki and me along, we could stop at all the speech clinics, psychology departments, and institutions for retarded children en route. We could spend a whole month looking for answers to our many questions.

For example, we could ask the speech specialists what they

would do with a child who had Viki's symptoms. At the age of thirty months she used only three words and these not always appropriately. In fact, some days she either refused or was unable to say anything. She used them best spontaneously in solicitation, worst when overmotivated or pushed. It had been hard for her to learn them and she did not say them in play as children do. We had proved that her vocal apparatus was capable of speech, that she could imitate certain sounds, and that her general intelligence was quite adequate. What was she lacking, we could ask the experts, and where do we go from here?

At the institutions for mentally-retarded children we hoped to learn of some type of child with Viki's two shortcomings— lack of language and hyperactivity. The people in charge of such children might teach us much about their training and management. We might gain foresight into what to avoid and what to expect in the future.

In the matter of intelligence testing, our colleagues predicted that Viki would not co-operate with a strange tester. Perhaps not, but if she did, and if she performed well on those tests which she had never had before, then we would have new confidence in the results.

At the two conventions and the various universities in our path, we might describe Viki's life and education and then ask what they would study, given this unique specimen. We could show Viki at work and play in one-way-vision observation rooms, wherever possible, and let them hear her words. After running her through her Imitation Series, we could invite them to suggest further items. We were always on the lookout for good ones.

Very soon we had talked ourselves thoroughly into The Trip. Our friends thought that we were insane and forecast dire mishaps as Viki expanded her enterprise to include the entire eastern half of the United States. Nevertheless we plunged into a month of feverish preparation.

Since Viki's vocalizations are subject to her moods and motivation, and since we wanted to be sure that the speech experts heard her utterances, Keith began preparing a sound movie with which to supplement our discussions. The frustration we experienced was not unlike our usual state when trying to film our unpredictable baby.

Renting sound camera equipment, Keith first attempted to record her reflex cries and barks. To produce an anger bark, I dressed her in an itchy woolen sweater which she usually tore off with the chimp equivalent of cusswords. But today it only tickled her, and she rolled on the floor, chuckling.

"Well, let's try to make her hoot," Keith said.

We delivered a mock scolding which customarily elicits her sassy hooting. But today she acted sweet and coy and very very silent.

Keith set his jaw. "We *can* make her *scream*, that's for sure," he said.

We tied her to a tree and walked away, adjusting the sound equipment to handle the earsplitting scream which was sure to come at any second now. Instead she began crying "Mama!" so plaintively that I scooped her into my arms, and we dropped that attempt, also.

The last chimp noise we tried to get was her food bark. I made a speech into the camera which concluded, "Approaching food causes Viki to give the typical chimpanzee food bark." Then I held out a cup of milk toward her.

Viki said, "Cup!"

At this point Keith decided that Viki was not "chimpy" enough to produce dependable reflex noises. He went over to the Laboratory and set up his apparatus opposite some caged animals. After several unsuccessful attempts to make them vocalize, he stomped off in disgust. When he was thirty feet away from the camera starter button, they began sounding off in chorus. He raced back to the camera, but by that time they were all sitting silently, staring at him. A "rat psychologist" at heart, Keith came home muttering dolefully, "With men who know chimpanzees best, it's white rats two to one."

Later when we ran off the film we made that day, it was found to be completely useless. Even those shots of her reflex and voluntary sounds in which Viki had co-operated were spoiled by defects in the equipment.

We enlisted the aid of Mr. Girden Russell, a professional photographer who specializes in sound movies. Once again Viki demonstrated her ability to perform at her best with strangers and in new situations. On several different afternoons Mr. Russell moved in with his impressive camera, eight hot lights, yards and yards of wiring, and either his wife or his son to assist him. Viki did not threaten their expensive equipment, and when they were ready, she vocalized promptly in the best of humor. The serious intent of Keith's introductions to each scene was somewhat blurred, however, by the grinning little ape who wriggled in his arms.

The Russells were fascinated by this assignment. As we finished each scene, Keith yelled, "Cut!" but Mr. Russell could not resist shooting a few more feet as Viki scooted up the blinds or disappeared into the kitchen in one spectacular leap. "Everything they do is funny," he explained.

In addition to the sound movie, we wanted to take along on our trip the complete photographic record of Viki's life. To bring our albums up to date, I spent many evenings in the Laboratory darkroom printing pictures. After they had dried on our table overnight, I pressed them in a book to take out the curl.

One morning Viki watched me doing this from her room. That afternoon I was trimming the margins on the photographs while Viki sat on the table claiming the scraps. Suddenly she began tucking these pieces one by one into the pressing book. When the scraps were all used up, she busied herself pressing the unanswered mail, various pages of manuscript, and the shopping lists from the kitchen bulletin board. At some unobserved moment the contents of my wallet went into the dictionary. As she was about to insert an envelope of cancelled checks, they spilled to the floor. With delighted little grunts, she picked them up one at a time and pressed them. When I was making dinner, I put down my pot holder for an instant and it, too, was whisked away to turn up later in the phone book. For the next week, Viki's squirrel compulsion kept us hopping, as if life in our house was not sufficiently confused at the moment.

Departure Day was set for April 16. All our thoughts and activities now pointed toward that day. Keith's extensive itinerary very soon accounted for every hour of our month away and only occasionally did he arrange to be in two places at the same time. Because of the nature of our family, he was anxious to ensure in advance a roof over our heads at each stop. In reply to his letters we received many hearty invitations from friends, institutions, universities, hospitals and motels. To our surprise, nearly everyone assumed that Viki would require special accommodations. We assured them that she would have her own bed, her own potty, and, tongue in cheek, that she would not be the slightest bother.

The days grew fewer. I prepared our clothing, reviewed all of Viki's schoolwork, and gathered a small satchel of toys to keep her amused in the car. Diaper washing would be a problem. Research revealed that gauze diapers dry in one-third the time of ordinary ones. Since she uses disposable paper liners, I planned to wash out each day's small laundry of diapers and dry them on whatever radiator or shower rack the night provided.

Friends dropped in to wish us well and shake their heads over us. When I served them coffee, Viki made a ritualistic little fuss over the coffeepot. She pecked at it with her lips brought to a point, and waved her hands over and around it. When her cup was empty, she held it under the spout, said, "Cup!" and looked as if she expected the coffee to flow.

Everything was going as smoothly as a Western Union clock until almost the last minute. Then, of course, I remembered a million things I had forgotten to do, and two of our best friends became engaged which called for a big celebration at our house. When the smoke cleared away it was Departure Day minus one.

On the very last day at home, I woke up with a sore throat and hardly any voice. We thought for a fleeting moment of canceling The Trip, but after all this preparation, I would have gone on the journey in an ambulance if necessary.

While I simultaneously cleaned mildew from our suitcases, stood for a suit fitting, and gave myself a Toni, Viki made her presence felt by following the dressmaker around my hemline, removing the pins as fast as they were inserted.

And then the little pest disappeared completely. With my head dripping wave solution and pins sticking into me, I ran around the house searching for her and calling in my croaking voice. Finally, as I glanced about our bedroom upstairs, I thought I saw the lid of one of our suitcases move a bit. I looked more closely. Slowly a slit opened up, and two brown eyes twinkled within. Then with a chuckle the occupant pulled the top down upon herself. At this point I hurried Viki down the stairs and into her room.

With great patience she watched me finish my permanent,

but when the wiry wet hair was released from the curlers, she insisted on being allowed to come and play with it. She likes to pull each curl straight and let it spring back into place.

To everyone's surprise, at eight o'clock that night we were ready to go. The Toni was under control, the suit was finished, the car was packed with a month's supply of clothes, diapers, and Chux. Viki's bag of toys rested on the floor under the dashboard. Photo albums and notebooks of data were available for inspection, and Keith sat smugly appraising his jam-packed schedule. But it was too good to be true.

Suddenly, from Viki's room, came the familiar sound of rending timbers. Viki had caught the excitement of preparation, and pounding within her crib, had broken off the top. Keith worked far into the night fixing it in the Laboratory shop. Meanwhile, I tried to put Viki to sleep on the couch with laryngitic lullabies, containing sudden passages where my lips kept moving, but no sound came out. With a voice like this I intended to ask speech experts, "Why is it that my little ape has so much trouble talking?"

CHAPTER 20.

They Loved Us at Vassar

AT NINE O'CLOCK the next morning, Keith said, "O.K., girls, let's put this show on the road." We were off on The Trip.

Viki bounced up and down on my lap, waving bye bye to Mrs. Clarke, and expressing her delight at going for a little ride. How was she to know that a month would pass before she again swung through the pecan trees?

Glad to be on our way, Keith raised his voice in song. I added my hoarse croaking, and Viki said "ahhh ah ah" with much energy and variety, thus making the first trio we had ever had on our travels.

We kept moving throughout a picnic lunch, so that it was noon and we were well into Georgia before we stopped at our first gas station and heard the first shout, "It's a monkey!"

The attendant offered the first comments and questions of The Trip. Putting myself in his place, all I saw was a baby chimpanzee in clothes, turning the steering wheel vigorously from side to side. Yet he said, "She can do anything but talk, can't she?"

We felt pretty silly about having just spent two-and-a-half years finding that out.

We drove through Georgia and into South Carolina. Our destination for the night was Charleston. If we had required many more filling station stops, we never would have made it. No sooner would we pull into one of these places than smiling, questioning people would descend upon us. "What *is* it?" they would ask, "What does she eat? How old is she? Where is her tail—curled up inside her diaper?"

To the latter I would reply that while monkeys have tails, apes do not. In fact, I would say, chimpanzees actually have fewer tail bones in the spine than people do. In the open-mouthed silence that followed this revelation, Viki and I would slip into the little room marked LADIES.

Each restroom presented Viki with a new bit of experience. One had a tile floor which inspired a little dance. Another had a push-button soap dispenser. A third had a chain pull on the potty, and still another had a full-length mirror on the inside of the door. When I closed it and Viki caught sight of a woman carrying a baby chimp, she clutched me and barked in surprise. Then she grinned as if embarrassed and slapped both me and the mirror.

Arriving in Charleston, we found our friend Jim Anliker in his lab at the Medical College of South Carolina. While we visited, Viki prowled around, exploring. She came upon a mounted human skeleton, and glanced up at it as if considering its arboreal possibilities, but she inhibited nicely. Her most appalling discovery at the college was their potty, which flushed steaming hot water!

We had no reservations in Charleston. Since it was very late, we decided to avoid complications by registering simply as a couple at the first motel. Concealed by the night, Keith carried in Viki's bed and I followed with her under my coat. We departed just as quietly in the morning, leaving the manager no reason to suspect that he had ever had a chimpanzee guest.

Around noon we left moss-draped South Carolina and entered clean windswept North Carolina. The sunniest part of the South was now behind us, and heating pipes ran from the floor to the ceiling of each Clean Restroom. Viki leaped from my arms and greeted the first of these as if it were her faraway pecan tree.

North Carolina is a beautiful place, but to Viki scenery only means that she will see fewer people. She spent the whole second day on the floor of the car, playing with her bag of toys.

We ate our lunch in a drive-in, before the interested gaze of Viki's public, answering questions between our hamburgers and French fries. The only new one was: If she had a husband like herself, educated and everything, would their children know all these things? I replied that Viki's children would no more inherit her learned skills than I inherited my mother's ability to milk cows.

We arrived in the late afternoon at Duke University. While Keith gave a little talk to the assembled psychology department, Viki romped about the room, and I made poorly timed efforts to capture her. She was tugging at the people, mussing their hair, and threatening their nylons, but since they kept saying, "Isn't she cute!" I stopped fussing. Apes and monkeys seem to hold a great fascination for people, and Viki has the additional appeals of being young and approachable.

Keith wanted to demonstrate her Imitation Series and her three words, but he had no food with which to bribe her. The audience obliged with candy, chewing gum, and an apple. The man behind me whispered to his companion, "Why doesn't he pass the hat?"

After our appearance one of the psychologists, Dr. Karl Zener, took us to his beautiful home, which overlooks a farm valley and a wooded creek. At dinner we established what was to be our eating procedure for the whole trip. Viki sat on my lap, and I fed both her and myself from my plate. As a result, I got very little to eat until she lay back in my arms like some contented heathen idol and fell asleep.

We spent this second night of The Trip in the Zener's guest cottage. Before putting Viki to bed, I sat by the fire brushing her. She stared into the crackling flames and said, "Blook! Blook!" When I had tucked her in, I rinsed out her day's diapers and draped them about the bathroom, while from inside her bed Viki still mumbled "Blook! Blook!" Then I fell into bed, weary in every muscle, and the last sound I heard was one soft "Blook!"

The next morning Viki was in a housewifey mood. She dusted the little house, wiped the windows, and swabbed out the wash basin. As we were leaving, I could not figure out how to turn off the lamp. Viki watched my efforts for a time, then reached up and pulled a certain knob, which I had assumed was merely ornamental. Keith saved my face by saying that she had seen him do it.

The third day out Viki settled down to exploring the car. She opened the windows and stirred the air with her long hands. She tested the strength of all seams and gadgets. She had to be taught not to help with the driving by hanging from the gearshift. She beat out jungle rhythms on the dashboard until we yearned to send her to her room. She began playing on top of her bed in the back seat, and then, to our great delight, we found that we could send her there by saying, "Go to your room!"

Mile after mile we flew over the highway, through North Carolina into Virginia, stopping for just one purpose. One Clean Restroom had a potty which had been stained by iron water. Our fastidious baby refused to use it. She did, however, recognize the possibilities of their continuous roller towel as a trapeze.

We had dinner in Washington, D.C., with Dr. Glen Finch, the psychologist who had home-raised a half brother of Viki's ten years earlier. While we compared notes, Viki raced around the room, letting off steam.

After dinner, we moved on into the night, through the permanent-looking national capital to geometric Baltimore, with its row after row of tall slim houses. Very late, we arrived at the home of the Goodspeeds where a party was in progress to greet us. Viki had quieted down by now. She looked about with big eyes as a dentist, a dermatologist, a psychologist, and others from Johns Hopkins asked questions about her, each according to his specialty.

Our hosts may have suspected that we were actually traveling with not one, but two, chimpanzees, for in the morning the little lady of the night before was replaced by a merry monkey who swung up the steam pipes with her gray corduroy skirt flying out behind her. She played their piano, too, in her own fashion, which consists of hard-fisted bangs interspersed with ever-so-soft tinkling notes—first the knuckles, then two fingers only—bang, bang, bang, tinkle, tinkle.

We sailed through the states fast now, on our way to Worcester, Massachusetts, for the meeting of the Eastern Psychological Association. Every time I looked at the highway signs, they proclaimed a new state—Maryland, Delaware, Pennsylvania. People were friendly here, in a folksy way. In Bridgeport we almost caused a riot when school kids surrounded the car and jammed traffic.

The road became narrow, winding through many small hamlets and even barnyards, and we kept getting lost in detours. We were impressed by the number of cemeteries here. Viki seized me in panic when tombstones sometimes appeared at the very edge of the highway on both sides. Keith reassured her. "It's the live ones you have to worry about, Viki."

Darkness found us somewhere in New Jersey, hungry but with no drive-in in sight. Since our home for the night was hours away, in a friend's apartment north of New York City, we decided to break our own rule by taking Viki into a diner. As we sat down in a booth, the proprietors grinned at us, but quickly stiffened their faces in the blasé manner of this metropolitan area. They served us without comment. With her big eyes just peeking over the table top, Viki stared at them, also without comment. Many customers came and went, never glancing our way, nor did the owners call attention to us. This pleasant anonymity continued until all the French fries and hamburgers were eaten, and we called for dessert. It was ice cream. One look, and Viki burst into such loud food barks as only ice cream can evoke. Heads straightened and turned all over the diner. Our privacy was at an end.

The next day we drove through the Hudson River-Palisades country, Viki's first mountains and her first interest in scenery. She spent the day on my lap, murmuring "Boo!" at sudden sweeping vistas of streams swirling past huge boulders. This was a rainy day, and Viki assumed the chore of operating the windshield wiper when needed.

At Danbury, Connecticut, we had stopped for a red light when a little boy came out of a store, carefully unwrapping a wad of bubble gum. He caught sight of Viki. Very slowly his face broke into a Christmas smile as he stared transfixed, and all the while his hand absently guided the bubble gum into his mouth.

The committee in charge of housing the convention at Worcester had been uncertain as to whether the Hayes family would require a room or a cage. So they placed us with the

Shaws, who happened to have both available. We rented the room, but politely declined the use of a cage in the animal hospital which they operate. Keith went off to the meeting at once while Viki and I stayed to visit with the Shaws.

They instantly fell in love with her, and laughed heartily as she ran around their house, bellyflopping on the beds. In their kitchen, she saw many new things—a bucket of coal, a gentle but terrifying polka-dot dog, and Dr. Shaw's rubbers. When he tried to put these on, although he was already wearing shoes, Viki looked up at him with a worried frown and tried her best to prevent him from making this obvious error.

Later, she fell asleep watching their television set, having first taken a disconcerting interest in the wrestling matches.

It was cold and crisp the next morning, and the men hurried in and out of the animal hospital in red-plaid mackinaws, like prints of Massachusetts—Early Spring. All the way up the eastern edge of our country, we had been experiencing spring in reverse—from bloomed-out Florida, through the bursting Carolinas, to budding New York. Here it was still winter, but Viki did not mind the chill air. The barren trees were all the better for climbing.

She also amused herself by running upright along a stone fence tumbling down the topmost rocks like something that doesn't love a wall. She had never seen stones in sandy Florida, so here she kept picking them up like great treasures, and carrying them to our room.

Since Keith had no meetings that afternoon, we went to nearby Boston to introduce Viki to an otolaryngologist. After a careful and exhaustive study of a defunct chimpanzee's pickled larynx, this man had published several papers, explaining that apes cannot speak because of their overcomplicated apparatus. Viki never said "mama," "papa," and "cup" better. She also made the sounds of her Imitation Series, and thor-

oughly examined both him and his office—all to the enchant-
ment of the good gay doctor.

Boston is said to be easily shocked, but we did not find it
so. When a boy who saw us became excited about "the
monkey," his elderly companion, who looked like Benjamin
Franklin, hastily set him straight. "It's just a child in a monkey
costume, of course," he said.

On the way back to Worcester, we bought two boxes of
chicken-in-the-rough. On the floor of our room, in the solid old
Yankee farmhouse, we had a picnic. Viki's sideburns were
charming, flecked with bits of drumstick and French fried
potatoes.

The following day was even colder. When we went out to
hang up the diaper wash, the apple trees were making brittle
sounds and Viki showed no interest in climbing them.

That afternoon we showed our movie and introduced Viki
to the convention at Clark University, and then we were ready
to move on to Vassar.

The next day was Sunday and we had now been away from
home for a whole week. On this cold New England day, I
suddenly realized that Viki had become toilet-trained. Keith
suggested that it might be self-defense, to avoid being washed
in the icy water.

At lunch, in a Connecticut drive-in, Viki went into her usual
song-and-dance, while we answered the usual questions, trying
to make the answers sound spontaneous: What does she eat?
(Oh, just the same as a kid.) How much does she weigh?
(Twenty-seven pounds.) Does she understand everything that
you say? (After I state her limitations, I demonstrate one of
her best comprehensions by asking her for a kiss. She pro-
trudes her lips toward me perfunctorily, but never takes her
eyes off her ever-loving audience).

At Vassar we were housed in the Alumnae House, in what the school newspaper called the bridal suite. These were elegant quarters, and once more Viki reacted to nice surroundings with a gentle touch. Most of the young ladies on the campus seemed to be entertaining week-end dates, mostly from Yale. The girls were poised, with a New York sophistication which had not quite jelled. When their young men, friendly and very much alive in the manner of Yale men, grinned at us and played with Viki, the girls relaxed also and then we noticed how very fresh and pretty they were.

That night I bathed Viki and brushed her to bring out every bit of her natural beauty. Then, remembering those girls on the campus, I fussed over myself far into the night.

April 25 was Viki's great day at Vassar. At nine o'clock our host, Professor L. J. Stone, ushered us into the observation room of his Child Study Department. Two walls of this soundproof room had large one-way windows. These looked like opaque mirrors from within, but permitted spectators to watch us from outside. All day long, movie cameramen recorded our activities through these windows, while Vassar students and faculty looked on. Since Viki had no idea that she was performing for an audience, her play behavior was natural, and the people saw a good sample of her everyday personality and her accomplishments.

Professor Stone periodically handed in toys which he had previously used in his studies of children. Balloons came first, and her play with these demonstrated motor activities such as running and jumping, her postures, and her emotional control. When the balloons inevitably broke, Viki was not unduly alarmed. She startled, glanced at me to see if it was all right, and then amused herself with the pieces. She played with additional balloons with Cameraman Josef Bohmer, batting them back and forth. She played ball with him, also, throwing a ball for the first time in her life.

Next Professor Stone gave us a box of miniature toys, and the audience saw Viki's curiosity, her surprising gentleness with small things, and how well she can manipulate in spite of her short thumb. She opened the doors and drawers of the tiny toy furniture and kissed miniature dolls whose mouths were only specks on the faces.

The next group of toys called her senses into play. The bells, the singing top, and the music box she used as she had her own at home; but she found the kaleidoscope a fascinating new toy. Next came a tangle of cellophane ribbon, which she dragged around behind her and dumped over her head in a silvery shower. However, our home-raised little ape would not accept Professor Stone's invitation to scribble with chalk on a tarpaulin rug.

After lunch we visited the playground of the Vassar nursery school. Viki made like a monkey on the swings and ladders and invited one and all to climb them with her. Not one, but practically all, did so. Then back to the observation room we went, for a session of testing. Once more, except for frequent trips to the potty down the hall, Viki was unaware of the crowd outside.

Mrs. Fiedler who conducted the examination corroborated our own findings on the Gesell tests. Viki's performance on other tests was dependent upon her experience with the principles involved. She did very well on the pegboards, since many of her toys involve the idea of putting things into holes. She was unable to solve the jigsaw puzzle, however—a principle utterly new to her.

Viki was a quiet hard-working subject. Not only did she co-operate with this stranger, but she even took her hand and guided it to the apparatus for additional demonstrations. Mrs.

Fiedler's handling of Viki was perfect—pleasant but reserved. Not until she playfully tickled the little ape did the test session turn into a block-throwing fracas. (Throughout our Trip we found that the tester's attitude greatly affected the results. Viki quickly took advantage of playful examiners, or those who gave her too many hints. In our travels, we met only one antagonistic tester, who ran her in a cold dark room late in the day, with much slapping down and snatching away of apparatus. Viki did little more than stare at this rude fellow as any properly brought-up young lady might.)

We left Vassar the next morning with the feeling that Viki had here enjoyed one of the most useful days of her life. And on the front steps of Alumnae House a row of ladies lined up to wave bye bye at us.

This was the day that Papa fell ill. I had by now settled into the spirit of the One Night Stand and all its inconveniences; and Viki, as you may well imagine, had never been happier, nor did she so much as sneeze during the whole of our time on the road. But now, as we drove over the Storm King Parkway, Keith complained of feeling tired and feverish. Our studies at Letchworth Village, a state institution for feeble-minded children, were cut short by his increasing symptoms. By dusk, his temperature had climbed to an alarming 103 degrees.

At that point I packed him into the car and with Viki clinging to me in a troubled sleep, I drove to Rockland State Hospital, to our good friend, Dr. Elaine Kinder, who always knows how to handle an emergency. She immediately sent Keith to bed and called in another doctor.

Meanwhile I made plans. I would put Keith on the first plane out of here and send him home, out of this cold and damp, and the hectic sort of carnival life we had been living. The doctor had other plans. He talked of viruses and things which would keep Keith in bed for at least four days. It looked as if The Trip had bogged down.

Dr. Kinder sprang into action. First she turned over to us her apartment at the hospital's Staff House, moving her essentials to a room down the hall, from whence she hovered over us like a guiding angel. Then she consulted a list of our engagements and obligations. We were scheduled to speak to the staff of this hospital the following morning, and since Viki and I were geared for action, we decided to carry on as well as we could without Keith.

Making sure that the patient was comfortable, Dr. Kinder glanced at her list once more, said she would call for us promptly at 10:17, and bade us good night.

The next morning, Viki was up early, staring at her oddly inert Papa, and peeking through the curtains at the doctors leaving Staff House, on their way to the hospital. Then we went into the dining room for breakfast. From her usual place on my lap, Viki shook hands with the doctors present, and paid the kitchen staff such compliments as they had never heard before—happy, chimpanzee food barks.

Promptly at 10:17, Dr. Kinder whisked us off to the staff meeting. It was not as formidable as I had anticipated. Only the questions of these many psychiatrists were disconcerting: Does Viki know she's a girl? (Our anatomy books are available to her. She does examine all parts of her body—using a mirror, if necessary.) Is her play more masculine or feminine? (What can you say about a tomboy who loves lacy petticoats?) Any Oedipus or Electra business? (No, I think that Viki loves Keith and me about equally well—or shows about the same degree of enlightened self-interest with either of us.) Has she shown any evidence of inferiority feelings? (Who? Viki?)

One of the doctors brought his little boy to Staff House at lunch time. The two youngsters wrestled happily in a big chair until Viki stumbled onto an embarrassing hold. The boy drew back from her, but his father smilingly reassured him, "She likes you! She likes you!"

After lunch, we settled Keith with a pile of mystery stories, a pitcher of orange juice, and his physician. Then Dr. Kinder, Viki, and I hit the Big Town.

At the Psychology Department of Columbia University, they had prepared a tea for us. A crowd gathered to watch Viki drink three cups, say her words, and amuse herself in the swivel chair of Dr. Henry Garrett. Then up and down the steam pipes she flew, making passes at the fedoras, shaking hands which were offered to her. She called up every sort of reaction from her audience. Some met her shyly, in the way grownups usually meet children. Others giggled as if they were on some daring lark. One patted my arm and said, "Oh, I think this is grand, what you're doing!" Another looked at us sideways with his eyebrow arched and said, "What exactly *are* you doing?"

I attempted to demonstrate the answer in their observation room, but Viki merely escaped into the hall and romped about the Child Guidance Clinic. A ferocious little boy pointed a toy gun at her and shouted, "I'll blow your head off!"

At which, a woman with a career-girl hairdo broke it up with, "Let us not mix the problem children and the chimpanzees, please!"

Next we trooped across a little public square, en route to our first batch of speech experts. The park looked like a *New Yorker* cover, complete with policemen, children, nursemaids and prams. Soon Viki had a retinue extending all the way back to Columbia, while shrill young voices called, "What *is* it, Mommy? Mommy, answer me, what *is* it?"

At Teachers College we met with about fifty speech specialists, and a pattern was formed which was later repeated at every speech clinic we visited. Holding Viki as I talked, I told them about our experiment, and showed our sound film. Afterward I had planned to ask the experts for advice. Instead, confronted with the bizarre sight of a word-saying chimpanzee, the experts bombarded me with questions: Can you speak chimpanzee with her? (Yes, we commonly call her to the table by making food barks. We can rearouse her interest in a "boo" place by saying "boo" and acting mystified.) Can you get her to make her sounds before a mirror? (Yes, she frequently plays at this.)

When I got a chance to ask for their prognosis, they were very encouraging. They liked the Imitation Series. One man thought he might use something similar with certain patients of his. They advised against pushing Viki. Let her tie down these three words before you confuse her with more, they said. They patted me on the back, said you're on the right track, and the meeting was over, leaving me happy, but not much wiser.

The following day I also rested. Viki played with Dr. Kinder's antique spinning wheel, scooted across the cement hall on a rug, and subjected the funiture to a stress and strain analysis.

Late in the afternoon Keith expressed a great desire for a root-beer float. Viki and I immediately set out to find the makings. After an hour's tour of the New York countryside, we finally came upon a little store. We entered without thinking how our appearance might upset the balance of such a place.

The long, lean Yankee storekeeper and his short, round woman leaped up from their potbelly stove and surrounded us with questions. They touched Viki, and they cautiously touched me, and they peered closely into our faces, as if to determine our planetary origin. Then they asked, "Is that a *real* chimpanzee?"

I said yes, but this only led them to stare harder and repeat the question. Finally the man went to the door and looked at our car. This seemed to reassure him. "They're from Florida, mother," he explained. "There's a lot of them down there."

I brought the conversation around to the subject of root beer. The man was scornful. Folks in these parts never touch the stuff, he said. All they carried was sarsaparilla. Then he resumed his studies of anthropoid anatomy until Viki began drawing back with resentful little barks.

Back at the hospital, while Keith drank his sarsaparilla float, he mumbled to himself, "What did they mean, is it a *real* chimpanzee?"

The next day, Viki and I drove to New Haven to visit our good friends, the Yerkes family. All the way there on the Merritt Parkway, cars would pass us, slow down until we passed them, then pass us again, all with much craning of necks.

In New Haven, our first stop was at Yale University Press. While we chatted in Editor Eugene Davidson's office, Viki played with his telephone. When I mentioned that Viki often dialed the operator, Mr. Davidson called the switchboard and asked the girl to disregard any calls from his office, since he had "a chimpanzee up here."

We spent the most relaxed evening of The Trip at the Yerkes home. Mrs. Yerkes noticed that between talking and feeding Viki, I was getting very little to eat. Therefore while I fed Viki, Mrs. Yerkes fed me; and then we talked and laughed until bedtime. I had not brought Viki's crib, but she proved to be a tolerable bed partner—once I had become inured to sudden jabs by her bony knees and elbows.

In the morning after breakfast, Professor Robert M. Yerkes, probably the world's foremost student of the chimpanzee, got down on the floor and played with his little guest. Then Mrs.

Yerkes danced her about the room, and their daughter, Roberta, held a flashlight so that Viki could see the cuckoo come out of the clock.

When we returned to Rockland Hospital, we were pleased to hear that Keith was much better, and that we could now continue The Trip. We moved on to Vineland, a training school for children "whose minds have not developed normally." Here, as at Letchworth Village, where Keith took sick, we were looking for some classification of mentally retarded child combining hyperactivity with lack of language. This would provide us with techniques for training and discipline as well as a prediction of future possibilities and limitations. But we were unsuccessful in our search.

Most of these children had very general deficiencies, and none behaved very much like Viki. Those with her degree of language trouble were extremely retarded in other fields, including motor skills. On the other hand, a child of six whose all-around intelligence has reached the level of a normal three-year-old, is still well ahead of Viki in speech and language understanding.

As to finding help with handling her exuberant personality, the Vineland children, who are very well cared for, are as gentle and well-mannered as most normal children.

Viki was rated on the Vineland Social Maturity Scale, which covers self care, locomotion, play—both independent and social—and communication. Viki was judged to be eight months ahead of the normal human her age, even though her total score was dragged down by a language development equal only to a one-year-old's.

While Dr. French looked on and instructed me, I gave Viki several other tests. She was surprisingly good at her first attempt to solve the Seguin ten-hole formboard, performing on this and the pegboards at about six months beyond her age. On most of the problems, however, she approximated a child of two-and-one-half years, with failures in the jigsaw puzzle and buttoning. She had never seen a jigsaw puzzle before Vassar, and I removed all the buttons from her clothes before she could swallow them. (When we returned home, I gave Viki a buttoning toy, and a two-piece jigsaw of plain wood. Within a week of occasional practice, she was a whiz at both.)

Viki was very difficult at this testing, leaping from the table and racing about the room. Dr. French assured me that he was used to this sort of thing, in the test situation. While we stood outside his building discussing the results, Viki ran away and climbed a tree. A group of the perennially young residents gathered to watch her tumble overhead. I tried frantically to get her down, bribing, coaxing, shouting, running away from her, and all the while our audience looked on with the sweet and pleasant smiles of those who will never know what a tough world it really is.

Leaving Vineland, we continued over the Westchester Ferry, and into the heart of industrial America. Around noon we reached the Pennsylvania Turnpike, which streaks across southern Pennsylvania, fast, wide, and straight, almost to Pittsburgh, our destination for the night. It is interrupted only by glorified gas stations, and we, of course, visited many of these. They continued to add to our education. Here there were paper seat covers, fluorescent sterilizers, and pedals on the floor to flush the potties. There were new examples of Homo sapiens, too, like the woman who shook hands with Viki and then visibly recoiled. "Her hand feels just like a human's. Gives me the creeps!"

I wondered what she expected a primate's hand to feel like —a sock full of wet sand?

I was coming to dread these stops, for the people who gathered around were often ill-mannered, pounding on the windows, shrieking, bringing out the worst in Viki. She accepts people on their own terms: if they expect her to act like a gay but mannerly little lady, she does so, but if they expect her to act like a wild animal, she certainly does not disappoint them.

At one of our Turnpike stops, Viki and I were in a cubicle when three girls came chattering into the washroom. I decided to wait for them to leave first. One of the girls entered the booth next to ours. Viki immediately tried to pound on the wall. I tried to restrain her, but she got one arm free and reached under the partition. There was a horror-stricken scream from the next booth, followed by, "My God! What's that!"

I snatched Viki to me and raced out of there, catching only a glimpse of the other two girls staring into the mirror with poised lipsticks.

We spent the night fourteen stories above Pittsburgh at the Western Psychiatric Institute. Our friend's apartment had an enclosed porch, where we let Viki run around barefoot to wear off some of her surplus energy. It took the next four days to remove the Pittsburgh soot from her feet.

Here, again, Viki amused herself with the telephone, picking up the receiver, listening for the click, and then putting back the instrument. Once the phone in the adjacent apartment began ringing. Viki snatched up our receiver and listened, her eyes in the direction of the ringing, and when it stopped, she gently replaced the receiver.

The next day we drove on, over the rocky hills of western Pennsylvania, a sliver of West Virginia, and the green hills of Ohio. In the afternoon we entered Michigan, where Viki and I had business at the University of Michigan while Keith went to Detroit to attend the convention of the Midwestern Psychological Association.

Since we had no reservations at Ann Arbor, we went from motel to motel, seeking shelter. At the first Viki entertained the manager's children while Keith talked to the man. When we found that all their cabins were reserved for the next few days, we moved on. The second manager stared at Viki, and then said that his place was being remodeled at present. At the third, a scrappy old man with a white stubble on his chin insisted that the "little fella" get out and box with him. We finally settled down in an out-of-the-way place near Ypsilanti.

An hour later, a friend in Ann Arbor tried to locate us by calling all the motels in the phone book. At the first place we had stopped, the manager cried, "An ape! Good Lord, my kids were playing with it! I thought it was just a little monkey."

Our friend decided to refer to us as the "people with the little monkey" on subsequent calls. The second manager we had seen said, "That was no monkey. That was a gorilla!"

The next morning, Keith ran some errands in downtown Ann Arbor while Viki and I waited in the car. A policeman came down the street, placidly strolling his beat. He spied Viki. He came over and talked to me, and he and Viki exchanged broad grins. Suddenly, for a reason I will never know, she said very loudly and distinctly, "Cup!"

The policeman straightened up. "She said, 'Cop'!" he exclaimed.

"She did?" I replied, amazed at his interpretation.

"Well, didn't you hear her? She said, 'Cop'! I'll be flat-footed!" And then eagerly, "Can she say anything else?"

Seeing that his standards were so lax, and his pleasure so genuine, I could not resist the temptation to shrug and say, "Oh, she says lots of things."

We visited the Psychology Department of the university and

their Bureau of Psychological Services. Here Viki dashed out of the playroom, and ran up and down the fire escape. People peered out at every floor, and hands reached out to grab her, but I finally had to climb out myself and stumble up and down in my high heels until I captured her.

On the way back to the motel, Keith waited with Viki while I ran into a restaurant to pick up some picnic materials. When I returned to the car, a young boy was posing again that old question: Is it a *real* chimpanzee?

Obeying an impulse, Keith said, "No, it's a fake!"

The boy just glared at him, and then turned to me. "Is it a *real* chimpanzee, lady?" When I said yes, he said gee, and walked away.

After our picnic, we fell across the bed, dead tired. Even Viki looked weary after three weeks away from home. Now, stretchy, contented, and full of f. f. potatoes, she joined us in a long long sleep.

The following day, while Keith went off to the convention, Viki and I visited the University of Michigan speech clinic. While we waited in the hall, a crowd of teachers, patients, and students of speech correction assembled. Someone gave Viki a sucker, to see how she used her tongue in licking. Two young men got down on their knees before us, to examine her teeth and lips. A pretty coed clasped her hands and said, "Isn't she the darlingest thing you ever saw?"

Suddenly a very surprising thing happened. An elderly lady came out of one of the offices, and as she passed us, she clucked her tongue and sighed, "Poor little captive creature!"

I could scarcely believe my ears. Could she mean Viki, secure on her mama's lap, licking a big lollipop, holding out her hands in greeting to an admiring throng? But the woman went on, "Poor little thing! Not where she's meant to be."

The question immediately arose as to whether she meant not

in the jungle, in the belly of a leopard, or not in a zoo cage. But the woman only sighed wanly and walked away.

At this speech clinic, they at last answered my question: What would you do if we brought a child with Viki's symptoms to you? They put her through the standard routine examination.

First, a little man with an air of enormous importance determined that she could indeed hear, and that her range of hearing was well within the normal range of speech.

Next they examined her mouth parts, and found no defects in her lips, tongue, palate, or teeth. They listened to all the sounds she could make, and saw all the mouth movements she was able to repeat after me. They saw that her words "papa" and "cup" are whispered, but by placing a hand on her throat they could feel that "mama" is voiced. They thought at first that she spoke on inspired breath, but when they put their hands before her mouth, they realized that she speaks as people do, on exhalation.

Their conclusion from all this, and from our testimony to her great difficulty and fluctuation in speaking and understanding, was that Viki did not speak because of a condition resembling human aphasia. In people, this is usually due to a brain abnormality caused by illness or injury. In chimpanzees, it is probably due to the lack of certain brain parts which have never evolved in that species.

The experts here then asked me what we had done so far. Then they advised me, as the other experts had, to keep at it.

Before we left Michigan, we met Dr. Kenneth Pike, a linguist in the Anthropology Department, who emphasized what may be called the building-block aspect of language. He pointed out that language is more than isolated words. It requires, for one thing, the recombining of words in a group to get an entirely different meaning. Dog bites man vs. man bites dog, to give a classical example. Would Viki be able to do this? Certainly not without a much larger vocabulary, but we could test her *comprehension* of such recombinations right now. She was excellent at the commands "Bring the dog!" and "Kiss me." When we got home, we must see if she would obey the new command "Kiss the dog."

We had only one more engagement. We had been invited to Indiana University by Dr. and Mrs. W. N. Kellogg, who studied the baby chimpanzee, Gua, about twenty years ago, and reported their results in the book *The Ape and the Child.* The campus was beautiful and bustling, the staff and students exceptionally intelligent, but our hearts were straining southward. One last time, Viki made merry in a professor's office, climbed up the heating pipes, pecked at his typewriter, snooped in his files, while a crowd looked on and laughed. We met one last speech expert. Without a look or a listen to Viki or us, he sallied into a lecture on how to teach a chimpanzee to talk. When at length he paused for breath, we murmured that, by some odd coincidence, this was exactly what we had done.

In the evening we showed our movie once more, described our work, and put Viki through her paces. Then we folded up our show and headed home.

By noon the next day, the green swells of Indiana had become hills, and we were in Kentucky. The ears on the horses were getting longer now, and we knew we were headed in the right direction.

There were no crowds or questions to slow us down in Tennessee. We told Viki that this was because it's not good mountain etiquette to ask questions.

We spent the last night out in a Chattanooga motel. As we

drove in, the manager pointed at Viki, and said, "What's that?"

Keith replied, as he had been doing this whole month, "This is our little girl. Furry, isn't she?"

Now came the question I always knew would someday follow his glib introduction. The man took Keith aside, and said in a solicitous whisper, "I hope you don't mind my asking about her," he nodded toward Viki, "but how did a thing like that happen?"

May 10 was a happy day, and we were up early and on our way. Viki sat between us quietly now, content to look about and wait. When Keith broke into song, Viki daintily pressed her wrist to his mouth, and after that he waited quietly, too.

In the afternoon the red hills of Georgia flattened into pecan groves and mile after mile of piney woods. And at 9:00 P.M. we were home.

CHAPTER 21.

Over the Fence and Off to Mrs. Clarke's

THE letdown feeling which followed our month of travel hit Viki the hardest of all. Up in her pecan tree, she gazed wistfully at the highway, straightening up as people or cars approached, but when they passed us by, settling down again with her chin on her hand. I strained my resources to give her all sorts of extra attentions, but I never quite managed to be a crowd.

After a few days of boredom, Viki returned our life to normal by reviving an old mischief—she began running away several times a day, usually to visit Mrs. Clarke. The matter reached critical proportions when we realized that we had no sure way of keeping her at home—or of getting her back once she had run off. Even my old trick of retrieving her by running toward home was no longer effective. In her present hunger for an audience, Viki would *rather* be with Mrs. Clarke —whose house overflowed with guests even more frequently than ours.

The problem had been with us for a long time. Even at eighteen months, she had occasionally gone calling by herself; but at that time she had always come home when we called her. It was when she began climbing trees that our real troubles started. For several months we had managed to get her down by threatening to come up after her. But one day Keith made the mistake of actually doing so. He went as far as he thought the branch would support him, and when Viki—still ten feet out of reach—saw his limitations, the trees became her unchallenged domain.

We tried to break her runaway habit by using the stick, only to realize once more the futility of punishment. I could not spank her *while* she was running away, and once she was up in a tree, my stick only made her more reluctant to come down. Spanking her after I got her home did not prevent her from running away again at the first opportunity. How could we convey to her the basic reason why she must stay close to us, the people who are responsible for her? How could we tell her about other gentle, trustworthy apes, who have brought about their own sad ends by taking little walks for themselves? Running away is a glamorous binge for a human being of any age, but it is a luxury in which no ape can afford to indulge.

We realized that eventually Viki would have to be fenced in for her own protection.

Early in June, Viki spent most of one day on the loose. It began when we went outside that morning. She ran over to Mrs. Clarke's garden. I ran after her, but with a head start she made it to the nearest tree. I told her to come down, clapping my hands sharply, in a way that sometimes carried weight. Now she only grinned and clapped her hands back at me. I decided to sit at the base of the tree and simply wait for her to descend. Fifteen minutes later she began sneaking down, but when I tried to grab her, up she went again. After an hour of this, I caught her, and marched her home and into her room.

But this was only the beginning. Before lunch that day she had run away four times—every time we went outside, in fact. I exhausted every trick I knew to get her home: I held up candy to her, and grabbed her as she reached for it. Once I pretended to find something of great interest on the trunk of the tree, and seized her as she came to look. I summoned her home on the run another time by starting the car.

In the afternoon I tried the love treatment. I had been standing under the redbud tree, promising her total annihilation in a loud voice. On a hunch I switched to sweet and gentle words. She slid down in a wink and covered my face with kisses. Then she leaped over my head and ran down the road, her little bowlegs churning like an egg beater.

A car turned into the Grove. My heart stood still as it came straight at her. She stopped, turned, and looked as if she were about to come to me. Instead she ran through the garden and disappeared into the bamboo thicket.

My knees were shaking and I was suddenly very tired. I fell into a lawn chair, from which I could watch the road and protect her from cars, if necessary. Then I waited for her to weary of her wandering.

An hour later, Viki came home. She carried a staff of bamboo, and over one ear hung a streamer of Spanish moss. She was covered from head to foot with sand and with slime from the fishpond. On her face was the good-natured, sheepish look of an alcoholic come home from an escapade, apologetic, and not quite sure of his welcome.

I cleaned her up and locked her in her room. Then I phoned Keith to say that the time for our fence was *now*.

The next morning, the sound of his hammer woke the Pecan Grove as Keith started building The Fence. Viki, a born sidewalk engineer, watched from her window, probably unaware that her wings were being clipped. As I watched beside her, I thought of other advantages to our fenced-in yard. Viki would no longer remove laundry from the washlines. Stray dogs, pigs, and snakes would not bother us. Neighbors less enthusiastic than Mrs. Clarke would be ensured their privacy.

The yard would measure about thirty by forty feet. Our house would form one side, and our back door would be the only entrance. Since Viki could scale any ordinary barrier, The Fence would consist of wires which carried a small electric charge—enough to be unpleasant, but not at all harmful.

After Keith had pounded in all the posts, he attached insulators to them and strung three strands of wire, ten inches apart, from post to post. Then he stretched chicken wire along the bottom so that Viki could not crawl under. Inside the yard he set up her swing, her pool, and a group of lawn chairs, which would be the focus of our outdoor life. The charger was installed near the back door, and then the job was finished. We sighed with relief. Now we were happy, and Viki was safe within our impenetrable fortress. But Mrs. Clarke just laughed. "I'd like to see that thing hold Viki!" she said.

No sooner was our little ape admitted to her new play yard than she headed for the wires. Keith yelled, "No! No!" but she did not stop. She grabbed the wire, and was startled by its jolt. She jumped back; but in a minute or two, she grabbed it again. Another shock. For the rest of the first day, she was very cautious. Papa had built The Fence, and she stuck close to him for protection from it.

The next day was another story. With her hair a-bristle, she launched a stick-throwing, foot-stamping attack against The Fence. Nothing happened. Next she waved her hands gracefully between the wires. Still nothing happened. She threw her ball out, waited for it to roll to a stop, and then broke into a little dance of triumph. Now, with her hands extended before her like a diver, she stuck her arms between the wires once, twice, three times, and alleyoop! she sailed through The Fence. When Mrs. Clarke saw Viki coming, she laughed long and loud.

This happened many times. Sometimes during her leap, Viki actually touched the wires, but since she was not grounded while sailing through the air, she was no more shocked than birds are when they sit on high tension wires. We were so impressed by her ingenuity, and the porpoiselike grace of her jump, that we set up the movie camera and recorded several escapes.

Then Keith added more wire, to prevent her from slipping through hereafter. We would have built a tighter fence to begin with, but we had expected one shock to discourage Viki. We had failed to reckon with her courage, and her enterprise when faced with a problem.

Having found one way out, Viki now made a thorough examination of The Fence. She slapped quickly at the chicken wire, and found that it carried no charge. She discovered that the posts were also shockless. Only the horizontal wires were connected to the current supply.

She glanced up at the low porch-roof over our back doorway. Then she climbed up the angle brace which supports it. Now, summoning all her energy, she shoved off from the house, hurling herself out into space—and over The Fence!

With a sigh Keith got out the large roll of wire with which he had thoughtfully provided himself, and electrified this area, too.

We went outside again. A lawn chair was standing very close to The Fence. Viki must have noticed it at the same instant I did. In two jack-rabbit hops, she was onto the chair and over the topmost wire.

We retrieved our baby, put all the equipment in the center of the yard, and hopefully sat down to wait. Now there was a gleam in Viki's eye as she ran along The Fence in her best puzzle-solving mood, tapping all the safe places.

"She's taking the wrong attitude," Keith complained. "She doesn't seem to understand about boundaries, and good fences making good neighbors. She just considers it a challenge!"

I held that with almost sixty combined years of experience and education as the chosen species, we two ought to be able to outsmart one little monkey. We decided on the spot to figure out how many ways *we* could get out of the yard, and then block those exits. We discovered seven:

1. Between the wires. (We had already spoiled this route.)
2. Over at the back-door roof. (Not any more!)
3. From the back of a lawn chair. (These chairs are so heavy that if we kept them well away from The Fence, we could interrupt any moves on her part.)
4. Tunnel underneath. (This also would take time, in which we could apprehend her.)
5. Push down the chicken wire, and squeeze through. (Keith immediately went and pulled this very taut and firm.)
6. Toss a piece of metal against The Fence, grounding the whole thing. (We were sure that she did not know this much physics, and hoped that she would not learn it by accident.)
7. Turn off the charger by flipping the switch at our back door. (We must not let her see us do this and touch The Fence in close succession.)

In conclusion we told ourselves that we should expect to be frustrated from time to time, by the very nature of our experiment. Any parent finds his child's education something of a boomerang. But at least our runaway problem was solved, we said.

While we talked Viki romped up and down, throwing sand at The Fence, rapping the posts with her knuckles, and kicking backward at the chicken wire like a very small donkey. Then she made a sassy hoot at us, and with a smug look on her face, plopped down on the ground with her back to The Fence. The ground happened to be damp. Her diaper was damp. And her back touched the wire. There was a crack of electricity, and Viki yelped and leaped into my arms. Some education comes hard, and now I was sure that the Battle of The Fence was over. Viki had been really upset by its sneak attack, and we had taken into account the seven possible exits.

The following day, Viki played happily in the sandbox, which we had just added to her yard. She completely ignored The Fence. Around noon Mrs. Clarke appeared in the distance. Viki sat on the edge of the sandbox, and ran her eyes slowly around the wires. Then she loped over to the corner of the house, where The Fence is attached. Narrow boards form this corner, and on these there was just a fingerhold. Up she climbed, hand over hand, foot over foot, stepping carefully between the wires. Then over and away!

That night I tried to break the news gently to Keith. "You know, Keith, this fence thing is a neat little study in itself. Informal, of course, but it reveals a lot about Viki, her problem-solving attitude—"

"What are you trying to tell me?" he asked suspiciously.

"Well, you know how clever she is, and how much The Fence challenges her? Well, Viki has discovered Escape Route Number Eight."

The next morning, Keith wired the corner of the house. When he was finished, he wiped his hands, saying, "So we can say there *were* eight ways to get out!" He headed for the garage with his roll of wire.

But Viki had another little job for him. She knew that the posts, which extended well above the wire, are free of shock. Now she grasped one of these with her hands, cautiously avoiding the wires. Her feet found a safe grip lower down. Touching only the part of the post between the wires, she climbed to the top of it, and leaped clear.

She joined Keith at the garage door. I heard him gasp, and then he shouted, "Nine!"

He returned with Viki, his roll of wire, and the movie camera. Once more he recorded her daring break. Once more he added wire to The Fence, this time running it along each post, from insulator to insulator. Then he turned The Fence back on. "Nine leaks, all patched," he said triumphantly. "And that's the end of that."

But a minute later, as he poked the wire with his screwdriver to test its charge, he was surprised to find that it carried no current. He walked around the yard, but found no loose connections. Puzzled he went indoors to see if the power had perhaps failed. As he opened the screen door, the grillwork of which Viki had been busily climbing upon, he was almost hit in the face by a dangling electrical plug.

Looking up, he saw an empty socket. Viki, from her perch atop the screen door, gave him a look of sober innocence. But from her hand hung the cord to the charger!

Clapping a hand to his forehead, Keith grasped the temporarily impotent Fence for support, and weakly called out, "Ten!"

CHAPTER 22.

Monkey See, Monkey Do

POPULAR tradition has made "to ape" synonymous with "to imitate." We wondered what basis in fact might lie behind this commonly accepted notion. Expert opinion varies, and the few serious attempts which have been made to evaluate the imitative ability of infrahuman primates have not clarified the issue. We hoped that by observing our subject Viki, both informally and in controlled situations, we might arrive at a more concrete answer.

Viki showed her first evidence of imitation at sixteen months of age, when she began crudely copying my household routine —dusting, washing dishes, pushing the vacuum cleaner about. In a very short time, however, we began to wish that Viki were not quite so enterprising. For instance, one day she claimed the grater from my lemon-pie-making residue, helped herself to a lemon from the refrigerator, and grated it all over the living-room rug.

As Viki grew, such imitative play became more frequent until every tool we used, every little action, was apt to result

181

in her attempts at duplication—hair brushing, fingernail filing, eyebrow tweezing, the use of a saw, a drill, a bottle opener, a pencil sharpener.

Sometimes she saw us using materials to which she would not have access until hours later. Nevertheless, by "delayed imitation," she must try her skill. One night she watched me dab furiously with a washcloth, trying to remove spilled milk from my skirt. The garment was left hanging in the bathroom, and Viki was shortly put to bed; but the next morning she took down the skirt, wet the washcloth, and rubbed at the spots.

In order to make a movie of her spontaneous play imitation, we demonstrated a new activity, while Viki and the movie camera looked on. First I pounded a wooden stake into the ground with a hammer. Then I pulled out the stake, laid down the materials, and stepped aside. Viki instantly picked up the hammer and pounded the stake into the ground.

Next I rubbed the stake with sandpaper. All eagerness, Viki took up this absolutely new material, and went to work. Long after we had finished our movie, she was still sanding. In fact, she went indoors and spent several hours sanding our furniture.

We had not been working with Viki for very long before we realized that she would probably not learn enough language to enable us to communicate extensively with her. We began searching for nonlanguage forms of communication, by which we might get our ideas across. Imitation came to mind as a quick and efficient means of letting Viki tap her teachers' store of information. It was not necessary to teach Viki to imitate; she had already done so in play. What we had to teach her was the meaning of the command "Do this!" so that she would imitate our actions even when they did not seem like fun to her, even when they seemed pointless.

There were seventy items in the Imitation Series, which extended from seventeen months almost to her third birthday. At first she needed much coaching, but after a while she began imitating most of the new items immediately. These were always things which she had previously learned to do in other situations: the sounds she made in play, for instance; or "mama," which she had learned to say without the help of imitation. After about two dozen problems, she occasionally copied our demonstrations of acts she had never done before, under any circumstances; and she was able to run through a list of "do this'es" as fast as we could present them to her.

Viki never enjoyed the items of the Imitation Series as she did imitating in play. As might be expected, her performance was not as spectacular as the spontaneous imitation we saw every day around the house. However, the Series was a good investment, for it did give Viki a tool which serves her in problem solving and which has already given her two words.

In an investigation like this, informal observation must be supplemented from time to time by formal experiments under planned and controlled conditions. As Viki approached three years of age, we devised a number of problems which she might solve by imitation. The apparatus was such that the solution was not apt to be "seen" by her until a clear demonstration was given. And the reward came from the apparatus itself, immediately upon solution.

To determine whether imitation is built into the animal or results from training, we also gave some of the problems to a caged chimpanzee of about Viki's age.

And to compare her performance roughly with that of human children, and also to guard against condemning Viki for failure on any problem which human children could not do either, we also tested four Orange Park youngsters on the same work.

Viki was tested at our house; the chimpanzee, Frans, worked at the Laboratory; and we enlisted the home and help of our friend Lyla Kleemeier, for presenting the problems to the children. Since they were all playmates of her little girl, Chrissie, Lyla was able to put them at ease and encourage their utmost effort.

We were skeptical about whether these children would cooperate, since they are not in the habit of working for reward—but we had nothing to worry about. They were completely entranced by our Rube Goldberg apparatus and by the prizes which they could win simply by watching our demonstrations closely.

Problem 1. This was a tunnel made of heavy screening, in the middle of which could be seen a gaily wrapped prize. Nearby lay a long stick.

The first subject, Chrissie, was given two minutes to see if she could figure it out for herself. When she told us that she could not get it, I asked, "Shall I show you?"

She nodded. I took the stick, inserted it into the tunnel, and poked out the reward. Then I rebaited the tunnel and gave her a second try. At first she only patted the wire and tried to put her hand in one end; then, all of a sudden, she picked up the stick and quickly earned her reward.

Her little friends, Alice and Kathy, also had to be shown. Then, after much fingering of the apparatus, and shy smiling at the experimenter, they solved as Chrissie had. All the little girls eagerly unwrapped their prizes and played happily. The sole boy subject, Alan, was so fascinated by the equipment itself that after he had earned his prize, he did not open it, but put it back into the tunnel and poked it out again and again.

Viki performed quite like the children, taking a similar length of time.

Frans, the Laboratory chimpanzee, was hopeless. No amount of demonstration helped him, although he wanted his reward of fruit very much. Later, the experimenter guided Frans' hand through the proper movements, thus going beyond demonstration, and aiding him to have the experience himself. This encouraged Frans to wriggle the stick aimlessly, if someone put it into the tunnel for him, but he never did learn to make it move in the right direction. This problem, therefore, told us nothing about his imitative ability. He could hardly be expected to learn by imitation what he could not learn by direct experience. (Other work has shown that because of his lack of experience with sticks, Frans is unable to solve even the most elementary problems which require the use of a stick as a tool.)

Problem 2. The prize was placed in a box with a glass door, but no visible means of opening it. The base of the box extended backward two feet to a pair of upright posts, between which stretched a taut string. Nearby lay a stick. The subject was required to stay at the front of the box.

Chrissie looked the situation over. Then she picked up the stick and tried to poke the prize out, as she had in the last problem. Failing this, she gave up, and I demonstrated how striking the taut string with the stick caused the door to fall open. Each of the children needed a couple of demonstrations to solve this harder problem.

Kathy, who has everything that Viki lacks in the way of verbal ability, proved to be a valuable subject, since she chattered constantly, thus providing us with a picture of the thinking processes of a human three-year-old, and a clue to the difficulties of each problem. During her struggle with the stick-and-string apparatus, she kept saying, How do you get this door open?" and "What is this stick for?"

Once more the boy, Alan, after solving the problem and winning a toy soldier, put it back into the box, slammed the door shut, and struck the string again to open it. He also tried to turn the gadget upside down, to examine the mechanism.

Viki solved this problem with one demonstration.

Frans was again frustrated by his ignorance of sticks. After many many demonstrations, he had still not earned his piece of fruit. When the apparatus was turned, so that he could reach the string with his hand, he began to play with it, and soon caused the box to open—apparently by accident. He saw the point immediately, and was thereafter able to open the box in this way; but he might have starved, had his nourishment depended on his use of the stick.

Problem 3. The reward was put in the same box, but it was re-rigged so that the string extended from a hole in the side of the box to one of the distant posts. There was no stick, but to one side of the box stood a lighted candle.

When Lyla saw this contrivance she shook her head and said, "What will you people think of next?"

We showed Chrissie that burning the string with the candle caused the door to fall open. She imitated this solution instantly. The other little girls did the same, with Kathy piping up, "There! Now I've got it!" as the string started burning.

Alan blew out the candle and trotted outside to play. An additional child, who was given this problem, lectured us on how her mother did not approve of her playing with fire.

Viki needed four demonstrations before she imitated our burning the string. Her main hindrance was her fascination with the candle itself. She waved her hands gracefully over the flame, and hopped around it in little Viki-be-nimble leaps.

Frans was omitted from this problem, since it seemed inadvisable to supply a caged ape with a lighted candle.

Problem 4. The lure was suspended from the ceiling in such a way that it could be knocked down by throwing a ball, which lay nearby.

The human children got the idea after one or two demonstrations, but their throwing was very clumsy. Questioning revealed that they were not encouraged to throw balls in the house. They imitated successfully, but their performances were limited by their motor skill.

Viki has had more ball play than most children her age, and her hands and arms are more developed physically; therefore, she was more impressive on this problem.

Frans also imitated Keith's throwing—not accurately, but well enough to show his intentions.

Problem 5. This time the lure was suspended, by a magnetic device, from a light fixture in the ceiling. Chrissie watched wide-eyed as I set up this problem and as I spelled out the solution for her mother's information: to get the reward, the children must f-l-i-p the l-i-g-h-t s-w-i-t-c-h.

The children and Viki, also, solved this task without much trouble. Kathy giggled, "Isn't this funny?"

Frans was, of course, totally unfamiliar with light switches. Therefore, before presenting this problem to him, Keith coached him on the elementals involved. Even so, after ten demonstrations, Frans had not yet earned his reward.

Problem 6. The box was used again. This time three levers protruded from an adjacent board. The door fell open when the subject pulled the levers in the sequence we demonstrated—1-2-3, 3-2-1, or 1-3-2.

We ran Viki first on this problem, and were very disappointed with her performance. She imitated the lever-pulling enthusiastically enough, but paid little attention to our sequence. When we tested the children, however, we found the idea of sequence to be very difficult for them, as well.

This problem had an interesting aftermath: To simplify construction of the apparatus, the levers were phony. The mechanism which really opened the box was a ring which hung from a string at the rear of the box. The experimenter's arm rested casually alongside the box. None of the subjects noticed the secret during the experiment.

One day, after we had abandoned the problem, the lever apparatus lay on our table, while I sat reading and Viki played around me. Suddenly I heard the familiar sound of the door falling open. I looked up. Viki was dancing in triumph on top of the problem box, while her hand still held the secret ring. Now she eased the door shut, and squatting before the levers, she pulled 1-2-3 and glanced at the door. Nothing happened. 3-2-1. Nothing happened. She began pulling levers helter-skelter in all possible combinations, but the door never opened. Then, in one light-footed hop, she was over the box and pulling the ring. Bang! The door fell open. She repeated the whole process several times, making pleasure noises whenever she once more solved the true puzzle. There was no toy or cookie in the box at this time. Here was experimentation for pure curiosity—the lifeblood of science.

The last child to whom we presented the levers was Kathy, and at the end of her session she also discovered the secret ring. Her pleasure was as great as Viki's, but she added a characteristically verbal comment, "Now I see what makes it open, see!"

The major finding of this series of problems was that Viki was able to do the various kinds of imitation approximately as well as the children. Since we used only one educated chimpanzee, our study is not offered as a quantitative evaluation of anthropoid imitative ability. But it does show that her species has the innate factors necessary to imitation. This was not true of speech, where no amount of training could make up for Viki's innate deficit.

Frans' poor performance, on the other hand, illustrates the futility of asking a young animal to imitate if the basic elements of the problem are beyond his grasp. His failure may have been due in part to lack of self-confidence. While Viki has had ample opportunity to discover that she can do many of the things that she sees us do, Frans is accustomed to seeing people do things which are impossible for him—largely because he has not had the opportunity to learn.

The importance to us of imitation cannot be overestimated. It is a pedagogical tool which is giving Viki many of the elementary features of cultural living. Thus we are able to compensate to some extent for her comparative lack of language: where we cannot *tell* her, we can often *show* her.

CHAPTER 23.

A Day in the Life of a "Three"

AUGUST 28, 1950, was Viki's third birthday. A detailed account of that day may serve as a summary of the troubles and triumphs of Viki's daily life.

At 8:00 A.M. Keith unlatched her crib and raised the top. Out sprang Viki, like a large furry ball. She dashed to the bathroom and onto the diaper-changing board. Keith unpinned her and she leaped to her potty, just in time.

Next Keith gave Viki her toothbrush and she brushed her teeth, making little pleasure barks over the appetizing tooth powder. Finally, she washed her face. Most of it received only a swipe of the cloth, but she stood on the rim of the washbasin and peered into the mirror, to give her eyebrow ridges an exaggerated share of attention. Her toilet completed, she was put into her room until breakfast was ready.

At 8:30 A.M. I came downstairs. Viki greeted me with a soft "uh uh uh uh" through her screen door. She watched me getting breakfast with mounting interest, until, by the time I set the tray on the coffee table, she was hopping up and down and banging on her door.

I opened it and out she burst with a rush. She bounded to the top of the radio, ricocheted off the couch and onto the desk, where she stood hooting her hello to the new day.

I held out a glass of orange juice and she took it daintily between her thumb and forefinger. I poured the coffee and handed a cup to Keith. Viki put down her glass, which was now empty, climbed to the arm of Keith's chair, said "Cup!" and then helped herself. I gave her a cup of coffee of her own. Drinking all the while, she wandered about the room, over chair rungs, under tables, up and down door jambs. When her cup was empty, she asked me for a refill by holding the cup under the spout of the coffee pot and saying, "Mama!" and then, "Cup!"

She carried her second cup of coffee to the desk, where she lay on one elbow and blew at her coffee to cool it. I passed a plate of doughnuts. Viki took one in each hand and dunked them.

At 9:00 A.M. the phone rang. While Keith talked, Viki stood on the table, one hand on his shoulder, glancing first at him and then at the phone. As he finished his conversation and started to hang up, she claimed the receiver and put it to her ear. She listened for a minute with a faraway look in her eyes. Then she made a Bronx cheer and hung up.

Jumping lightly from the table, she picked up her red wooden box and put it over her head. Since it covers her whole face, this box makes good blindman's buff equipment. She ambled about the room, bumping into things and chuckling. Unfortunately, she bumped into her juice glass, and it fell to the floor with a crash.

She snatched the box from her head and clung to me, looking shamefaced. I put her into her room while I gathered up the broken glass, and in the confusion, Keith escaped to the quiet of the Laboratory.

At 9:15 A.M. Viki and I went to the garage to do the washing. She stood beside the tub, watching my every movement, and "helping" by dousing the clothes up and down, and rubbing them on the washboard. But when she lifted them high in the air to suck out the soapy water, I cried, "No! No!" She hooted at me and climbed up the wall. Straddling a rafter, she lay silently, staring at me.

When I started the rinsing process, she scrambled down. She is a real help here, since her strong hands can wring the laundry drier than mine are able to. However, when we had finished wringing, and I was ready to hang up the clothes, she wiped her sandy feet on them. "Oh, Viki, look what you've done!" I wailed, apparently sounding more distressed than I had intended, for she put her arms around me and kissed me thoroughly.

Then she ran off, and returned a second later with the spray gun. She took the cap off, held the sprayer under the faucet to fill it with water, screwed the cap back on, and sprayed the garage floor.

By 10:00 A.M. we were finished with the washing, and went inside to do our housework. To cheer us along, I turned on the radio. As I squatted before the dial, Viki jumped to the top of the cabinet, placed her hands on my head, and leapfrogged over me. When I started to get up, she pushed me down again, so that she could have one more leap. Then, as I walked away, she tuned out the station, and when I stooped down to adjust it, she took still another jump.

Viki helped me carry the trash to the garbage pit for burning, she pushed a dust mop around her own room, and when I started to wash her bed and its waterproof mattress, she took the cloth away from me, and climbed in to do the job right. Finally she performed her one regular chore: she washed the bathroom mirror and soap dish, rubbing so vigorously that the paper toweling disintegrated.

At 11:00 A.M. it was time for Viki to "go to school." As I took the equipment from the hall cabinet, she grinned and guided me to our work table with eager little barks.

First we worked on our six-piece jigsaw puzzle. Viki assembled it correctly without much trouble.

Next I put paper and crayons before her. She scribbled enthusiastically enough, but made no effort to copy my marks, although she had been imitating my housework all morning. She paid no attention either when I drew a border and told her to keep her scribble inside of the line. (I'm sure that she could do these things, if she knew what I wanted, but I cannot figure out how to get this idea across to her. It would be so simple with language! Her little friend Chrissie recently visited her older brother's school. There the children taunted her about being "too little to stay inside the line." Chrissie worked feverishly until she had mastered the idea.)

Next I gave Viki some tasks aimed at improving her dexterity. At "school" on her third birthday she built towers and bridges of tiny dice. She also threaded a needle, worked a spring paper clip, and scribbled with a pencil the size of a match in a miniature notebook.

12:00 noon was Viki's lunchtime. (She now eats breakfast and dinner with us, as a child would, but at lunch she is still working for food.) On her third birthday, we built matching towers. She imitated my selection of blocks without error. When instead of a tower I built a train of three dissimilar blocks, she selected three matching ones from the jumble before her and assembled them in the same order as mine. Finally I built a three-block tower without letting her see my construction work. When I showed it to her, she immediately selected the correct blocks, and stacked them to match my finished model.

At 12:15 P.M. we were ready to go out into the yard. (This play space now serves its purpose well, since Viki seems to have given up her ambition to break out of The Fence—at least temporarily.) Viki made a dash for her swing, which we have recently suspended from the only tree in the yard. She chinned herself on the elevated bar, and climbed the ropes; then she came to me, and taking me by the hand, led me to it. There she climbed to the bar and sat waiting to be pushed.

After I had pushed her for a while, she ran to a nearby lawn chair and climbed up on it. She waited expectantly, eight feet from the swing, until I fulfilled my part of this popular game by swinging the bar toward her. She leaped off into space, and with perfect timing grabbed the approaching bar and flew through the air on it.

Bored with the swing, Viki went to the sandbox. The first thing she did was to "plant" a weed. I was very impressed with the way she carefully pressed the sand around it until I remembered that she had recently seen Mrs. Clarke planting some young seedlings.

Now Viki began an entirely new activity. Bending over from the waist, she made an impression of her hand in the sand, and then deepened the print with her finger. She made a print of her foot, too, and while so doing she seemed to notice for the first time that her toes wiggle all as one while her fingers can move independently. She plunked down on the sand and studied this phenomenon. She found that she could grasp the toes and move one at a time, but on their own, they would act only as a team. But this seemed to be pretty deep stuff for a three-year-old chimpanzee; she jumped up from the sand all of a sudden, and raced madly around the yard.

She was interrupted by a car driving up to Mrs. Clarke's house. She sat on the edge of her sandbox, clapping her hands and calling to the people. They waved to her, but did not come over. She went back to the sand. Scooping up a handful, she stirred it into the rain water which had collected in her coaster. She then brought a handful of this mixture and lovingly patted it onto the top of my head. We hurried indoors.

While I cleaned the mud out of my hair, Viki washed her hands vigorously.

At 1:00 P.M. we returned to the yard to play with balloons. (Viki is very destructive of rubber balls. Therefore, in the interests of economy and habit formation, I am giving her several balloons every day. She plays with them as she does with balls, but when she bites a balloon, she loses her gay and lively companion in one bang. Perhaps in time she will thus be shown what we cannot tell her, and we can resume our various games with the more expensive balls.)

On her birthday, when Viki had broken the last of the balloons, she looked forlorn. Picking up the fragments of one, she put the mouthpiece to my lips. I showed her that it was no good, and tossed it away. It landed on the wires of The Fence. Viki approached it cautiously. Then she took my hand and led me to the place. She tried to make me touch the balloon, although she herself avoided The Fence.

At 1:30 P.M. I brought out the typewriter to bring Viki's diary up to date. She immediately planted herself between me and the machine. It was a very hot day, but I have grown used to her furry little self against me. I did not even mind when she bit hunks out of my carbon paper; but when she began snatching each type arm as it flew up, I chased her away. She hooted at me sassily and took it out on her sand bucket. Laying it on its side, she stomped it flat. Then, with a grin, she came back to me, to help some more with the typing.

By 2:30 P.M. I had finished the notes and lay back in a lawn chair to rest. Viki sat on the arm of my chair and we gazed out toward the highway together. Suddenly she startled and said, "Boo!"

Following her gaze, I saw that beyond the Grove, across the road, in the middle of the town's cemetery, a golden spot of sunshine was falling through a gap in the overcast sky. As we watched, the break in the cloud came toward us, leaving the cemetery clearing a black hole, while the trees between the clearing and the road were suddenly a shining curtain of Spanish moss. Next the road became a silver ribbon with the trees as a somber backdrop. Viki's "boo" became higher, almost shrill. The sunny spot came slowly toward us, and one by one the pecan trees were flecked with sunshine. Viki's arm gently circled my neck, and when a second later we were warmed by the dazzling sun, her "boo" had dropped to an awestruck murmur.

At 3:00 P.M. we took our bath. Viki submitted bravely to the soaping process, but her real pleasure came afterward, as she played in the water and rinsed herself with the spray.

At 3:30 P.M. we went to Viki's room to play. I proposed our old game "Go get the dog!" without noticing that the toy was not in sight. Nevertheless she went in search of it. For five busy minutes, she dug through her box of blocks, looked under the couch, and even under the rug. Finally, she emerged dusty and triumphant from behind her crib, holding up her toy dog.

After a session of this game, I tried to interest her in block construction. She ignored me until I incorporated some toy cars into my elevated highway structure. Then she pushed the cars back and forth for about ten minutes.

At 4:00 P.M. I told Viki that she must play by herself now, while I prepared the birthday cake and the dinner. As I closed her screen door, she galloped off to her mirror, where she sat examining her teeth and making play sounds like "ahhh," "tsk," and "kkkkkk."

Next I heard her pounding at her toy workbench, where she has mastered the hammer and nail, the claw hammer, the screw driver, and the nut and bolt. (The other toys available to her at all times in her room include a tricycle, stuffed animals, a toy telephone, blocks, and various educational toys. Only these are rugged enough to withstand her vigorous play. Things like clay, painting and sewing equipment, jigsaw puzzles, and the plastic animals of her toy farm are given to her only when we can observe and supervise her play.)

At 4:15 P.M. I went to her room again, to let her come and beat the cake batter, one of her favorite chores. But I found her asleep on top of her crib, lying on her stomach, with the dog clutched in her arms. (Short naps before or after dinner are her only daytime sleeping.)

I glanced about her room and noticed an odd structure in one corner. She had built a tall arch with two blocks on each side and a fifth block across the top. Later, we saw her making sounds into her toy phone and then holding it toward this structure. Keith hypothesized that she was hanging up the phone. I thought it might be her "baby" whom she was letting "listen." But she never told us what it really was.

At 5:00 P.M. I heard a commotion in Viki's room. She was pounding at the windows, and hooting. Papa was home!

I let her out and she jumped up and down as he opened the door. Then, in a wink, she was onto his shoulders and ready for a piggyback ride.

When I called them to the table, Viki slipped into her chair. She drank some milk, ate a forkful of asparagus, bit the buttered top off her roll, and then ran off, munching on a frankfurter. She ran to her room, where she got her dog, placed it upon her shoulders, and paraded past us—giving it a piggyback ride.

When Keith and I pushed back our chairs to leave the

table, Viki leaped to her place and polished off her plate quickly.

6:00 P.M. Enter the birthday cake! Viki went wild at the sight of it, jumping around the room and sputtering food barks. (To her this was probably just another cake—as this whole day had lacked special significance. On the other hand, Chrissie had anticipated her recent third birthday for weeks. Chrissie can also give a rather explicit account of what the birthday celebrates. Viki may never know about birth until she herself witnesses it or experiences it.)

By 6:30 P.M. Viki was full of cake. She gently returned her empty plate to the coffee table and went to the telephone. She held the receiver to her ear for a while, and then frantically dialed several numbers. (Her dialing is completely random, but occasionally she does call an actual number.) Suddenly, now, she stopped dialing and said "Boo!" At the same time we heard a faraway voice calling, "Hello! Hello!" I murmured apologies and hung up.

By 7:00 P.M. I had cleared away the dishes and was ready for the evening's entertainment. I gathered up a supply of clean diapers and Viki's blanket. Viki began making pleasure barks of anticipation. And when Keith asked, "Viki, do you want to go to the show?" she raced to the door, all gay and ready to go. In the car, she bounded from the front seat, to the back seat, to the place behind the wheel, which she energetically turned back and forth.

At the drive-in theater, she made excited little yelps as her beloved public peeked in the windows and laughed at her antics. The little boy in the next car saw her sitting a-straddle my open window and insisted that he be allowed to sit in the window of his car. His father complied with small enthusiasm.

First came the color cartoon, always fascinating, and then

a newsreel, which featured a gymnastic contest. Viki commented freely on the performance of the athletes who did many of her best tricks.

When the main feature started, she turned her attention to the adjacent cars. To our right were two middle-aged ladies who stared at her silently. She found the car on the left more rewarding. This carful of children and grownups whispered "Psst!" to get her attention. She obliged by blowing spit bubbles at them.

At 8:00 P.M. the screen resounded with a duel, complete with clashing swords. Viki attended carefully to this part. When the hero raised a glass of wine, to toast his fallen foe, Viki said, "Cup!" I decided that it was time for refreshments.

At the refreshment stand, a little girl, about Viki's age, told me a very unlikely story: "I saw a little furry baby," she said. "Back there, the man had a furry baby in a pink dress."

Her mother looked embarrassed and said, "As we passed one of the cars, she saw a monkey inside and she was simply fascinated. Calls it a 'furry baby.' I can't imagine why she singled you out to tell this tale to. I'm sorry."

"Guess I look like the gullible type," I said.

Returning to the car, I found Keith in a stew. "Will you please hold her a minute? I'm trying to light a cigarette and she keeps blowing out my lighter."

Viki drank her soda pop, helping herself to handfuls of popcorn from our family box. Then she went to the back seat and became very quiet.

At 8:30 P.M. I glanced back, expecting to see her asleep. Instead, she was at the window, making faces. Her audience was five little children who sat crosslegged on the ground, silent as Indians as they looked at her.

Now Viki climbed into my lap and put my hand on her ribs. I tickled her. She chuckled. I stopped, and she put my hand back on her ribs, pushing it suggestively until I tickled some more. Then, all of a sudden, she was asleep.

At 9:30 P.M. we prepared to leave. The intermission lights had gone on, causing Viki to jump up and look about. Now, for the first time, the two ladies in the car to our right spoke, "She's very beautiful, isn't she?"

I agreed that by chimpanzee standards, she is indeed a fine specimen. "But her eyes!" one of the women said, "Those eyes would be beautiful in any species."

It was 10:30 P.M. when we arrived home, and Viki was too sleepy to wait for her bedtime cocoa. She curled up on the couch and closed her eyes. When I asked, "Don't you want to say goodnight to Papa?" she flipped her hand a few times and let it fall to her side. I picked her up then, and took her to her crib.

Viki's third birthday was a very ordinary day in her life, and her activities were quite typical of this period. We have seen that, except for language, she is still quite similar in abilities to the child of this age. We realize, however, that her interests are a little different, more athletic, less verbal.

We have seen also that the advantage of language is much more than a mere chattering of words. Even at this early age of three years, the child, through language, is gaining more information, inspiration, and direction from adults than we could hope to give Viki.

We may consider intelligence as made up of three components:

1. The individual is born with a certain amount of *innate capacity*, and our experiment establishes this one fact at least: Until three years of age, the only obvious and important deficit in the ape's innate intelligence, as compared with man's, is a missing facility for using and understanding language.

Viki visits Mrs. Clarke

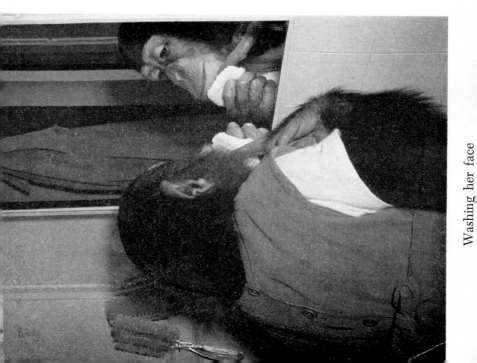

Washing her face

She develops dexterity with dice towers

Asking ("cup") for more cocoa, at her bedtime "party"

A house makes a fine gymnasium

She likes to listen to watches

One day she put her ear to a picture of a watch

2. The *personal experience* component of intelligence is what the individual learns for himself, motor and manipulatory skills, basic perceptions, social interplay, the elementary stunts of getting along in our civilized jungle. Viki has done very well in this respect. Exposed to the life of a child, she has absorbed about as much, through personal experience alone, as a child could.

3. But there is a third element of intelligence—*group intelligence*. Through language, the individual at a very early age begins to acquire knowledge secondhand from teachers, books, and daily communication with other people, infinitely more knowledge than he could ever gain through personal experience. Language conveys not only information, but ideals, traditions, and abstract philosophy. It fosters that cumulative thing—invention. It enables the mechanic and the mathematician to make use of each other's skills. And this has been going on for thousands of years in man.

This aspect of our intellectual life is so characteristic of our species that we take it very much for granted, and seldom appreciate how mentally ineffective each of us would be if we had to function strictly as individuals. Much has been made of the human brain's ability to cope with any change in our environment. But no one man, isolated from birth, could do this very well. It is man's collective brain, working over the centuries, which has made us increasingly versatile. It is man's unique ability to communicate knowledge which has led to that peculiarly human product, civilization.

Since apes do not acquire language to any significant extent—not even privileged apes like Viki, who are coached intensively on it, and who could profit a great deal by it—it seems unlikely that apes ever have or ever will develop a civilization.

Our Viki has tapped our cultural store of knowledge to an impressive degree, but the child of three has greater access to it. Year by year, Viki will continue to learn as much as we can communicate to her, but without language, communication will be difficult.

Upon man's innate capacity for using language depends not only the growth of civilization, but perhaps its very survival. For instance, if my lamp were to go out at this moment, I would first of all replace the bulb. If my lamp remained dark, but the other lamps in the room were on, I would examine the switch or the socket. If I saw any irregularities, I would repair them—after consulting a more informed human or a book, in all probability, for while I am very ignorant personally, almost every accomplishment of the human race is available to me in the world's massive accumulation of literature.

If all the lights in the room went out, I would replace a fuse, and if this did not remedy the matter, I would assume the trouble to be a power failure. The idea of trouble-shooting in a power plant appalls me, but if it suddenly became my responsibility, I'm sure I could find some books which would tell me what to do.

Now what would happen if the world were to be populated only by apes, each as educated as Viki is likely to be by adulthood? What would Viki do if her lamp went out? Being a bulb-snatcher of long standing, she might (accidentally or with some insight) remove a defective bulb and replace it with a sound one. This is as far as her training now goes. We could show her how to replace a fuse, by imitation, or how to repair a plug, or a socket, or a switch. We might even set up an elaborate training program, showing her how to test all these trouble spots in a logical order. But there is not time enough to teach her, in this way, even a small portion of what the child is simply *told*.

And some things cannot be communicated by any amount of demonstration or personal experience. If the trouble with Viki's light lay in the power plant, there would be no hope of her resolving it. How could she be given the idea of electricity, of its being generated, and coming from a distant place? Left in the hands of the most supereducated apes imaginable, our civilization would fall to pieces. One by one, the lights of the world would go out.

PART 3.

In Answer to Your Questions—

A CHIMPANZEE masquerading as a child is the sort of thing that naturally arouses curiosity. During the first three years of this experiment, we have met many new friends through Viki, and have had the privilege of answering many questions about apes in general and Viki in particular. Several of these queries are made so often that I am enlarging upon them in the following pages. In the order they will be discussed:

Is she very destructive?

What does she eat?

How does she take to wearing clothes and shoes?

Does she understand everything that you say?

Just how much of a *chimp* is she after all this?

How long will you be able to keep her?

CHAPTER 24.

Cagemates

A MAN'S home is said to be his palace, but if he chooses to share that home with an ape, it rapidly assumes many aspects of a cage.

The chimpanzee is, by nature, superactive and extra strong. Add to this a young animal in the process of being educated, of having its curiosity constantly aroused, and the house must change its face often to provide for its inmates. Only by making specific arrangements, preferably before trouble arises, can the welfare of the chimpanzee and the sanity of its human cagemates be preserved.

Our household witnessed such an adjustment in what may be called The Affair of the Vanishing Drapes. In the very beginning, our windows were bordered by drapes, which hung clear to the floor in graceful folds. But, at four months of age, Viki began using them to pull herself erect. Thus, early in our experiment, a decision had to be made. Since Viki was too young to realize that her tugging would eventually drag down the entire drapery hardware, the answer was obvious. I snipped the drapes to window-sill length, and out of Viki's

reach—for two months. Then she began pulling herself up to
the window sills, using the drapes like jungle vines. Again
I hacked them off, this time to midwindow. The final lopping-
off occurred months later, when she entered her Social
Phase. Performing for visitors in the front window, she would
often swing, Tarzan fashion, from one short drape to the
other. At that point, I reduced them to a mere valance across
the top of the windows.

Luckily we are not house-proud people, so that we were able
to dismantle our house one step ahead of Viki without reluctance. In the interests of our experiment, we aimed at simplicity,
thus minimizing Viki's inhibitory and our disciplinary problems. A youngster should not be expected to remember a long
list of taboo items. Too many homes are kept so nice that
children feel unwelcome. As everyone knows, this leads to
nights in the pool hall and juvenile delinquency, evils to be
avoided at all costs.

One by one, we removed from our house such accessories as
we could do without; and Viki turned her attention to what
remained. When she began cutting teeth on the furniture, we
took up the traditional chant of parents, "No! No!" Viki obeyed
instantly, and for just about an instant. Then she resumed her
gnawing. We doctored the scars, and revised our standards of
elegance.

As the infant Viki grew, more and more of our house was
exposed to her. She discovered towels, pillows, and bedding,
to drag around the house and out into the yard. There was
stuffed furniture for bouncing upon, chair rungs to climb over
and under, mirrors to make faces at, open drawers upon which
to chin herself, but especially, there were doors. She was
fascinated the day she learned how to operate them. At first
there were a few unpleasant moments, when she slammed a

door shut only to find that she was in one room and I was in another. She soon devised a simple precaution. She would start a door swinging shut, and race for the opening on all fours. Just before it closed, she would stick her head in the crack. Then with her head and shoulders, she would push the door wide open, and repeat the whole process. Her precious hands were never used in this game, only her coconut head, that part of her body for which she seemed to have the least respect.

By the time she was a year old, Viki was familiar, not only with doors and drawers, but with latches as well, and there was no hiding any part of the house or its equipment from her. Nor did we try to isolate her from most of our belongings. The mere business of living in a house is an education in itself. Viki's home is her classroom as well as her playhouse. Here she learned to use many tools and utensils, and a wealth of mechanical principles. What if she did scribble on the walls with lipstick, bars of soap, and raw shrimp? It all washes off, and scribbling is not to be discouraged. And if she went about turning on the lamps, water faucets, and radio, what of it? Manipulation is one of the things that places primates above the lower animals.

But then Viki began climbing. This brought our pictures within her range. She entertained herself by swinging them faster and faster until they flew from the wall. She took to sailing through the air from one height to another, and we made a point of arranging our possessions as if we expected an earthquake any minute. I doubt if the mountains of Ecuador ever shook harder than our tables do when Viki lands upon them from the tops of window casings.

One lamp lay directly in the path of Viki's favorite leap. Since a young chimpanzee does not consider the value of a lamp before she takes off into space, we secured it to the table with a C-clamp. Thereafter, we took secret pleasure in hearing our friends gasp, as Viki flew through the air from couch to table to chair, without once upsetting the lamp.

When Viki discovered the innocent intoxication of whirling in a circle, this also took its toll on our goods. She pirouetted on table tops, arms outstretched, sweeping aside everything in range.

As I tried to make our bed, she crawled under the covers, pacing around and around, pulling out the corners as fast as I tucked them in.

She was the death of one braided rug. She would put her finger in a loop of the rug's surface, and slowly rotate until her finger was caught. Then she would cry for "mama" to come and cut her loose. Loop by loop, I was forced to cut my rug apart.

One day she unwound a spool of thread among three rooms of furniture, and in a grand finale whirled until she herself was trussed up like a mummy. She squirmed and bit at her bonds, and finally came to me, hopping like a contestant in a sack race. Against my better judgment, I cut her loose.

With every day in our house, Viki's curiosity, genius for mischief and just plain monkeyshines increased. She learned to bulb-snatch, to raid my filing cabinet, to core apples with her whistle, and to fingerpaint on the rugs with butter and orange juice. My baking suffered when Viki discovered the thermostat knob, which controls the oven temperature, and which, incidently, makes a little light go off and on.

When imitation came into her life, the house was even more valuable to Viki as a school. She had always tagged behind us, dragging a pillow, to plunk down periodically and watch our activities. Now, in addition to watching, she imitated what she saw. This taught her many things, but it had its sad repercussions, as does every new skill she learns. For instance, after seeing me clean upholstery with cleaning fluid, she continued to dab at the spot with the next solution she saw me use—which happened to be floor wax!

By the time she was two years old, Viki's exuberance and enterprise had become supplemented with a great deal of strength. Sometimes while testing her muscles, she threatened the very existence of the Hayes house.

When she played tug-of-war with a certain pipe in the bathroom, I was kept busy with rags for hours until the plumber arrived.

In one prying action of her strong teeth, she could tear a plastic switch plate from the wall.

Several weekly shopping lists included panes of window glass.

When she leaped right through a screen, to get out and join Mrs. Clarke, our happy-go-lucky landlady said, "Oh, don't worry; they're very old screens." But that did not keep out the bugs.

We were in a constant state of repair. Instead of wielding the usual tools of our trade—pencil, stop watch, and data sheets—we were kept busy with sewing basket and screw driver.

The result was Viki's room. The rug on the floor and the comfortable couch give this pleasant sunny room a cozy atmosphere, but a second glance reveals the built-in furniture and the heavy screening over the windows. Perhaps because we are under no strain there, we find ourselves joining Viki in her room during inclement weather.

If she is in a reasonably calm mood, and we are free to keep an eye on her, Viki still has the run of the house. At these times, her agility saves her from many mishaps, and only an occasional "Gently!" is needed to keep her under control. The sort of gentleness which she accords old people and babies she is also capable of using with fragile objects, such as cups, glasses, or anything else we protect with our warning "Careful! Careful!" But there are a few things, among them toy balloons, which challenge her by their fragility. These we cannot protect except by removing them from her presence.

Raising an ape in a house is a rugged proposition, but it can be done, if the nature of the chimpanzee is constantly taken into account. To match the animal's athletic vigor, the house must be stout and functional. To minimize the animal's need to inhibit, the house must be kept simple, since, with its shortage of language comprehension, the chimpanzee must accept the taboos imposed by its human companions as a matter of faith without understanding why. Things of historic or sentimental value had best be packed away, for without language the chimpanzee cannot be expected to appreciate them. Above all, the household equipment should be relatively expendable, since the cost of replacements will mean no more to the chimpanzee than the threat, "If you break that lamp, you will not get a new tricycle for Christmas."

A visitor pointed out recently the extent to which we have sacrificed elegance. With a wave of her gloved hand at the tables bare of trinkets, at the clamped-down lamp, and the mere fringes of drapes, she asked, "Do you live here, too—or is this just where you keep the ape?"

CHAPTER 25.

Percomorphum and Pablum Milkshakes

FOOD preferences among the various breeds of man are determined largely by what they are taught to eat as children in each particular culture. So it is with chimpanzees. In the jungle they eat vegetation, fruit and berries in season, an occasional bug. At the Laboratory they are fed a carefully planned diet of milk, eggs, bananas, grain, and beans, as well as raw and cooked vegetables. And Viki, having been adopted into a human home, eats the usual foods prescribed for children of preschool age.

Apparently attitudes toward food are also learned, for Viki presents her human companions with the identical problems which most parents face in trying to make big folks out of their little ones. Viki's characteristic attitude toward eating is childishly capricious and indifferent, and she is every bit as finicky as the people she lives with.

Like most youngsters she has an inordinate love of sweets, a distaste for cooked vegetables, and such a tiny capacity that

I suspect some process like photosynthesis of contributing to her nourishment. Viki displays the same perplexing hunger strikes as the human child, the fluctuating passion and revulsion for milk, the exasperating playfulness as she dillydallies over her meal. She prefers to eat on the run so that her dinnertime has all the calm serenity of the feature race at Hialeah. Sudden unaccountable food preferences appear from time to time. Some days she dines exclusively on pork and beans, for example, or watermelon, or marshmallows, or laundry starch, or green onions and radishes. She drinks soy sauce straight from the bottle, my only objection being that when spilled on diapers, soy sauce leaves a stain which is impossible to remove. Like most people, she enjoys food which is fun to eat. She slurps in a strand of spaghetti with much noise and vigor until the tail end slaps her face with a resounding smack. The only cereals she accepts are the puffed varieties which "bang!," "crackle!" and "pop!" She stares fascinated during this crispy, crackly business, and says "Boo!" repeatedly, but she will not start eating until the puffed grains lie still and soggy.

A far cry from her present sophisticated apathy toward food, Viki started life with the infant's dedication to the bottle. Her diet was copied from that of her young kinfolk at the Laboratory, which in turn is similar to the human baby's. A very efficient sucker, she imbibed quantities of milk formula and orange juice through the standard bottle and nipple arrangement. She had to be burped after eating like any infant, and when hiccups resulted from her ravenous appetite, she had to be held aloft by the arms for a few seconds until she recovered.

In time Pablum was added to her menu. She rejected it with the familiar "square mouth" of human gagging, made by drawing the lips back into a rectangle. By three months of age, she was sucking Pablum eagerly from a spoon, however, and now mashed banana won her heart.

By four months of age, she was noticing people around her, and her interest became more intense if they were engaged in her favorite pastime, eating. If I was holding her on my lap while I ate—and in those "chimpy" days I was always holding her—she empathized every bite, her mouth absent-mindedly opening and closing in time with mine. She begged for a sample of everything by smacking her lips and making food barks.

Over the months many new foods were incorporated into her diet—diced bananas, strained vegetables, solids like zwieback, apples, and raw celery. She ate it all with the dainty nibbles of a lady mouse. But milk might more appropriately have been served to her in a trough. She was so fond of it that, if the bottle was held outside her reach, she pulled her hair and went into a tantrum. One day she found an isolated nipple on the couch, and bent over it with food barks of anticipation. When no milk was forthcoming, she bounded up and down on all fours, screaming.

One of Viki's major differences from the child in the home situation is that she has had to work for food from her earliest infancy. This was necessary to our experiment, for to understate the facts, we were not as interested in making Viki big and strong as we were in educating her. Since food is the basic incentive which forces an animal to work—be it a rat in a maze or papa going to the office every morning—we encourage Viki to learn things she might not otherwise acquire by giving her food as a reward. In the early days before she had enough teeth or technique to eat solid food efficiently, I plied her with Pablum "milkshakes" during her work sessions. Three times daily she drank these mixtures of milk, Pablum, percomorphum, vitamins, and either mashed banana, strained carrots, or other baby foods. Repulsive as this sounds, Viki worked enthusiastically for each portion: pulling strings, saying "mama," or whatever the problem might be.

When she was six months old, Viki was given her first poached egg. She accepted a spoonful tentatively, held it in her mouth for a while with a noncommittal expression on her face, and then let it slowly dribble down her front. But she accepted a second spoonful, and holding it out on the tip of her tongue, stared at it down the slope of her flat chimp face. This suggested possibilities to her. With the egg still balanced on her outstretched tongue, she suddenly whipped her head around in an arc, decorating the room and her mama. This happened many times.

I therefore began incorporating eggs into more solid and tasty dishes like custard. Ever since then, custard has been Viki's most consistently favorite food. I doubt if we could have accomplished large blocks of her education without it. Whenever a new problem is given to her, Viki goes on a hunger strike, or rather she refuses to work for fear that she will make a mistake. A batch of baked custards will usually see her over this hump of resistance, and she quickly masters the task and regains her appetite.

If Viki is a fair example, chimpanzees are not necessarily vegetarian. More to test this hypothesis than because we considered meat to have any unique value, we offered Viki strained meats when she was seven months old. She rejected these amorphous canned concoctions with the haughty scorn of a true gourmet. She selected meats from our table instead. She prefers sweet-flavored meats like ham, bacon, and corned beef. She also likes fat and raw meat. When I am cleaning chicken, fish, or shrimp, she begs for a raw tidbit, helping herself when no one is looking. She greeted an especially scary little visitor brandishing a large uncooked chicken leg.

From time to time Viki supplements her diet with various inedibles like buttons and cellophane. She also forages outdoors, eating flowers, leaves, and pecans. However she is not as self-sufficient as one visitor implied. Looking up at the bare branches of the pecan trees one wintry day, the youngster asked, "Does she climb the trees for bananas and coconuts?"

On the whole Viki's diet is quite like any child's of two or three years—lots of milk, eggs, fruit, and vegetables. She eats with a spoon, and drinks from a cup or through a straw. When her meal is over, she uses her napkin with the same engaging awkwardness as a young human learning the stunts of being grownup.

CHAPTER 26.

What a Funny Place for a Toe!

WE DECIDED in the first place that Viki would have to wear clothes for that most primitive of reasons—warmth. Considering that we enjoy a subtropical climate and that she came into the world complete with fur coat, perhaps a more important reason is psychological. Seeing her in clothes is a constant reminder to those about her to treat her like a child. This has proved so effective that our colleagues, who spend their working hours with caged apes, express embarrassment when Viki appears in their midst not quite dressed.

Viki's wardrobe is very simple and practical. During the stifling summer months, she wears only the basic garment— training panties, if I am free to watch for her warning signals, otherwise, diapers. As the weather turns cool, a knit T-shirt is added. For dress-up occasions, this diaper-T-shirt ensemble is topped by either a cotton pinafore or a corduroy jumper, depending on the temperature. Few other garments are required: a poplin windbreaker for outdoor play when the breeze is strong, sleepers for rare cold snaps, and a chenille housecoat to slip on after her bath and on chilly mornings.

A child's size four now fits her perfectly except for the sleeve length, and since she insists that all sleeves be cut short, this is no problem. In fact, there have been no problems in clothing Viki. With a chimpanzee's native love of self-decoration, she actually finds pleasure in her wardrobe. She often amuses herself by rummaging through her drawer and dressing herself in odd assortments of clothes.

We can claim no such luck in the matter of shoes, for we never did solve the problem of how to shoe a chimpanzee. The trouble lies in the curious chimp foot, which is remarkably well-suited for climbing trees, but very ill-adapted to the wearing of human shoes. It is exceptionally long and slender, with four small toes out front, and, projecting to one side, an enormous muscular big toe. Since this big toe is able to touch the inner surfaces of the other toes, much as our thumb can press against our fingertips, the chimp foot is a grasping organ similar to the human hand. In reality one could say that the chimpanzee has four hands.

This might be considered enviable except that buying shoes for a chimpanzee is like trying to find shoes to fit the human hand. Keeping Viki comfortably shod has been a constantly urgent tax on our ingenuity.

There were many reasons why we felt that she should wear shoes. It is particularly easy in this region to pick up hookworm through the bare feet. Also, we had a misguided notion that shoes would inhibit her chimpanzee impulse to climb. Finally, having her grabby toes bound, she might have been expected to grasp exclusively with her hands, thus acquiring greater manipulatory skill.

Viki wore standard baby bootees until at four months of age her feet were larger than the largest infant's. Not realizing at the time how unsuitable store-bought leather shoes would be, I went to a children's shoestore. I withheld the true nature of my baby, not in order that I might enjoy a private joke, but because I was a little embarrassed by our experiment and afraid that telling people about Viki would mean the end of my privacy. I simply asked the clerk for a flexible shoe or slipper for my four-month-old baby who was "confined at home."

Since I did not know her size, he asked me to mark the length of Viki's foot on his ruler. When the ruler recommended a size which is normally worn by two-year-olds, the man exclaimed, "Did you say *four months*? Shaking his head, he went off to get the first offering.

It was a stern little brogan with iron-stiff soles. I protested that it would hurt her "little feet," and he proceeded to outline the theories behind the shoeing of children. He said that "scientists" have worked out the only logical shape for the human foot. Sturdy "training shoes" were especially advisable for Viki in view of her heavy weight, as indicated by her large feet.

"Oh, she's not heavy," I interrupted. "She weighs only nine pounds." This set the pace for the whole interview. If the man was surprised by her big feet, he was astonished by her light weight. No sooner had I confirmed his guess that she had narrow, very narrow feet, than I insisted on the widest shoe in the house. I hastened to explain about her big toe sticking out to the side, causing him to stare pointedly at my feet.

One after another I rejected the shoes he offered. Finally he brought a pair which was a little softer than the others, and so wide they were almost square. In pity for the salesman, I bought this pair.

At home I slipped the shoes on a puzzled Viki. When I put her on the floor she stood as still as a statue until I moved away. Then she followed as fast as she could, screaming as only a frightened ape can, her arms and legs striking out at all angles as if from a series of internal explosions. We decided to let Viki's feet grow without the benefit of "scientific" guidance. But the problem remained of how to keep them covered.

Grandma came to the rescue by knitting extra large bootees for Viki. Our little ape presented a terrific view from the rear as she walked upright, the little bowlegs in the fuzzy woolen boots and her lowslung bottom wagging in a fascinating way. As each pair wore thin, I sent Grandma the latest sketch of Viki's foot, and she invariably replied with a new pair and the comment: "My, what a funny place for a toe!"

Viki wore Grandma bootees until she was eighteen months old, at which time her big toe would poke through the side in only one week. Two weeks left an irreparable tangle of shredded wool. Keith's mother also took to knitting bootees, but Viki, in a twelve-hour day of running, dancing, and biting at her feet, was wearing them out faster than the ladies could knit. It was obvious that stouter homemade shoes would have to be built.

From his Boy Scout days Keith had retained an admiration for Ojibway moccasins. These Indians cut their shoes from one flexible piece of leather which gathers about an instep tongue, leaving ample toe room. They cover the ankles, and the ties are knotted so that neither a baby Ojibway nor a baby chimpanzee could get them off.

With leather reclaimed from an old purse, I turned out a sturdy pair which lasted a whole month. I was delighted, but where was I to get more leather?

I went to all the hobby shops, shoe-repair supply houses, and harness and saddle shops in Jacksonville trying to buy some, but the leather merchants insisted that to cut into a hide would ruin it. I would have to buy a whole cow or nothing. They reminded me of the restaurateur who advertised steaks from every animal in existence. To the first person who ordered a rhinoceros steak, the waiter said, "Sorry. We can't cut up our rhinoceros for one steak."

At the last place I visited, the proprietor was very pleasant until I stated my business, "I'd like to make my little girl a pair of leather moccasins."

He immediately looked imposed-upon. He whined that if he sold me part of a skin, no one else would want the remnant. With great reluctance he showed me his treasures, many expanses of leather in shades of green, red, and blue. I quickly set my heart on a red goatskin, and visions arose of little red shoes climbing up the rainpipe. He was determined not to cut into it, but in the end, protesting bitterly, he split the hide in two. He refused to be comforted by my observation that the survival value of a red goat was probably not very good anyway.

Viki adored her red shoes from the start. The first day she kept sitting down suddenly to pat them. She arched her foot, apparently enjoying the squeak of new leather, and at dinner she could scarcely eat, what with looking under the table at her shoes. But with these, as with their predecessors, she was happiest of all when we came indoors and the shoes could be taken off.

I was able to cut three pairs of moccasins from the goatskin, and that carried Viki through the age of thirty months. By that time, she was going through them faster than I could sew on patches. I once more began a search for stronger yet comfortable shoes for Viki.

Our final effort was tennis shoes. Since these accommodate the chimpanzee's big toe, are readily available, and cannot be easily removed by the wearer, tennis shoes have become standard footwear for well-dressed show chimpanzees. Since Viki's feet were now big enough to be fitted with tennis shoes, I bought her a pair.

She rejected them with screams, and although they were plenty large and flexible, when we forced them upon her, she bit them, yanked them off and hurled them across the room. At this point we re-examined our motives for insisting that she wear shoes.

There was no further need to worry about hookworm, since The Fence keeps out the animals which carry the parasite. Shoes had not stopped her from climbing; with or without bound feet Viki can climb any furniture, door, or window frame which offers a sliver of a grip. Finally, although Viki has become very clever with her hands, she can manipulate almost as well with her feet in spite of three years of shoes.

And, since people who live with chimpanzees have problems enough without looking for trouble, we therefore abruptly dropped the whole question of shoes.

CHAPTER 27.

Actions and Words

OF ALL the questions we are asked by new acquaintances, the one we dread most to hear is: "How many words does Viki understand?" A definite answer is next to impossible for a number of reasons: (1) Failure to obey a command is no test of comprehension in our contrary Viki. (2) She understands in a fluctuating way—some days she "knows" a word perfectly, other days not at all. (3) Any list of understood words can be endlessly lengthened by including variations of the basic form. (4) Almost any expression includes a great deal more than the words themselves; and these other elements of the language complex—situation, gesture, the inflection, pitch, and loudness of the speaker's voice—are so bound up with the words as we commonly use them, that it is very hard to say for sure just what an animal (or a person) is responding to.

An example of this difficulty may be seen in the ritual by which Viki visits the bathroom: Glancing at the clock, I say, "Viki, it's time to go to the bathroom. GO to the BATHROOM."

Viki reluctantly heads for the little room, crawling over and under furniture on the way, tumbling and doing somersaults.

Eventually, in spite of all her stalling, she arrives at the bathroom door. Then I give the second command, "Get UP on the BOARD."

She climbs onto the diaper-changing board, which lies across the bathtub, and plays with the contents of the soapdish until I say, "Lie down, Viki!"

She lies down, I unpin her. If she is clean, I say, "Get over on your potty," and she steps from the rim of the tub to the potty.

When a suitable time has elapsed or action has taken place, I tell her to "FLUSH the toilet," "get over on the board," and "lie down." Then I ask her to "GIVE me a PIN." When she is securely fastened, I say, "Turn off the LIGHT." She does so and we leave the bathroom. Now I give the final command. Viki is by now busy with some toy, but when I say, "Close the door," she returns to the bathroom door and slams it emphatically shut.

At first glance this performance seems to involve considerable language comprehension; but on second thought we wonder if she might not be simply following a set routine. Would not a string of brusque but uninformative "Hup!'s" be enough to run her through this series of activities? When we test this possibility, we find that this is indeed the case. But it's not that simple either: if I now switch the order of the various items—tell her to get on the potty *before* I remove her diaper, or ask her to give me her pins while she is still on the potty—she does obey these *inappropriate* commands. She is hesitant, however, and searches my face, as if puzzled by the conflict between my words and the requirements of the situation.

On the other hand, when she is inattentive, she does the thing which makes sense at the time, apparently not noticing that I have asked for something else. (I also do this when a person's words do not match the situation. The fact that Viki does it more often probably reflects her low level of interest in language.)

There are some cases where we see no evidence of comprehension unless our words fit the situation. For instance, at bedtime Viki has a cup of cocoa, which we refer to as her "party." When we say, "Is it time for a party?" Viki makes food barks and heads for the kitchen. If we dally, she may get the can of cocoa from the pantry by herself. However, it is hard to say whether she is reacting to our words or has simply acquired a sense of the day's routine events. Certainly if I ask her if she wants a party at any other time of the day, she simply stares at me.

Early in the evening, we sometimes say, "Do you want to go to the SHOW?" With great excitement, she dashes to the front door, and into the car. But here also, there are other clues than the words. There is the time of day again, and also the fact that we begin turning off the lamps, and gathering up extra diapers, sweaters, and so on. Testing her, we find that she gives the show-going reaction only at the appropriate time of day. At nine o'clock in the morning, however, our invitation draws a blank stare. (I must admit that if I were invited to a movie at nine o'clock in the morning, I might also stare blankly.)

We have seen that the *situation* sometimes gives Viki a clue as to what we are asking of her. She responds to numerous other spoken words where understanding may depend on still other cues. For instance, a number of *sharp* words get her instant attention. Said with urgency, "Look!" or "Hey!" cause her to look first at us, and then at the object to which we are pointing or which has captured our gaze.

Better than any scolding is a *scornful* "You bad girl!" Impatient with her table manners, I mutter, "Stupid little ape!" She puts down her fork, looks in my eyes with a great sadness, and steals into my arms.

Sometimes *loudness* seems to be the only criterion for obedience. For instance, the words "come" or "come here" are ignored if uttered conversationally. Said with the slightest smile, "come" starts a game of tag in which I am constantly "it." I chase her round and round the furniture, up and down the house, while she slithers out of reach like a wet football. Finally, when she completely exasperates me by scuttling under the bed, I bellow, "COME!" Then she comes.

She often seems ignorant or deaf to a certain command until a sharp "Viki!" brings a delayed but proper response. When I complain that it is hard to say whether Viki *can't* or *won't* understand, Keith reminds me that, in either case, chimps are not selectively bred for obedience to verbal commands, as are horses, dogs, and people.

Are there any words which Viki comprehends without need of supplementary cues? There are a few, though the list is limited by her youth and her chimpanzee language deficit. She obeys the commands: "GO to your ROOM," "GO OUTSIDE," and "GO UPSTAIRS" without error. She will bring a cup when we tell her to. If she removes a taboo object from its proper place, we say, "PUT it BACK!" and she does so immediately and gently. She will "turn on the LIGHT" or "turn on the WATER," but may turn them off instead, if they happen to be on already. When told to, she will go find her shirt and put it on. If someone says "Goodbye" or "Bye bye," Viki waves. I depend on the command "GIVE it to me!" to get pins, buttons and scissors away from her. She obeys this even when we are not holding out our hands to receive the object.

As far as we are concerned, the most important word in Viki's vocabulary is "No!" We first used this expression when she was six months old, and books were her favorite teething rings. As Viki grew larger and our patience wore thin, the variations of "No! No!" to be heard in our house were limited only by her genius for mischief and our invective vocabulary. There came to be "Don't do this" and "Don't do that" for specific crimes, a low menacing, "Vikiiii," a rapid-fire "Hey hey hey hey," and between clenched teeeth, "Viki, I'm warning you!" More elaborate "No! No!" variations include: "Viki, get off those blinds before you pull them down and brain your papa!" "Must you bulb-snatch from every lamp in the house?" and "Don't flush the soap down the potty, dear."

Her typical response to all varieties of "No! No!" is to cease her sinning abruptly. Sometimes she throws herself prone and rocks. Again she will stamp her foot and sass us back. Most often she makes us feel silly by diverting her attention to something else, and listening in wide-eyed innocence to our rebukes, since she is obviously busy on another matter. Once the coast is clear, she returns to her favorite mischief (which is currently pounding on the windows with her feet, while she swings from the blinds).

When an object is delicate, but not forbidden, we calm her sudden bursts of animal spirits with "GENTLY!" or "CAREFUL!" She does not inhibit completely at these commands, but merely calms down.

If she is impatient to have a thing which we are making ready, we say, "WAIT!" and she waits patiently until we break the spell with "Here you are!" Here again, since "waiting" is basically inhibiting of activity, we consider it merely another shade of "No! No!"

From time to time we have tried to speed Viki's education by *teaching* her the meanings of words. Our greatest success, and that which has proved the most valuable to Viki as an experimental animal, has been "DO THIS!" We believe that she had a certain amount of imitative ability in the first place, and that we were able to direct and enhance it by teaching her to follow our "Do this!"

On the whole, however, we have found it even harder to teach her language understanding than to test it. After more than eighteen months of coaching, we have not yet taught Viki to identify her nose, ears, eyes, hands and feet. Some days, to be sure, she can point to all these parts without error, but at other times, she is completely lost. When we try to teach her a few new words, she may start to learn them; but then, suddenly, she can't even remember the old ones. Too many words apparently lead to confusion—and for Viki, a very few are too many.

In contrast to the artificial situation of identifying her parts, Viki reacts very dependably to certain words used in play. She always brings her toy dog when we say, "GO get your DOG!" even if it is out of sight in the next room. When we say, "LISTEN!" she bends an ear to the nearest wrist watch. "KISS me" is enthusiastically obeyed, although she does not always honor the proper parent when we say "Kiss mama," or "Kiss papa." In language comprehension, as in most of Viki's behavior, situations which combine motor activity and social interplay are the most successful.

By now it should be clear why we dread the question: How many words does she understand? Ruling out as much as we can of situation, gestures, glances, and inflection, and taking

Viki at her most obedient, I should estimate that she understands not more than fifty word groupings in the form of expressions or commands.

However, we allow the possibility that we may be underestimating her powers as we often do in other areas. Incidents like the following occur quite frequently. One night Keith found himself without a receptacle for his cigarette ashes. Trying to be funny, he said, "Hand me an ashtray, will you, Viki?" And she did.

To give a second example, on our trip we met a man named Carnochan who had collected apes in Africa. Within Viki's hearing he told us about his chimps who picked pockets with their feet. Later as I was showing him our photo albums, Viki amazed me with an entirely new trick. With her hands in plain sight and the glaze of innocence in her eyes, she reached out and snatched a picture with one chimpy foot.

Although Viki is generally poor at understanding words, she recognizes a surprising number of nonlanguage sounds. When a cap is removed from a bottle of coke, the fizzing noise draws food barks from the next room. At the first metallic swish of a lipstick being opened, she comes running for her sample. When we first began to play our "bring-me-the-dog" game, she simply stared at the word "dog," but when we barked, "Rhow! Rhow!" she ran straight to the toy.

Perhaps the thing that makes it difficult for her to learn words is that this type of symbol is not typically a discrete sound, but rather a combination of several basic sound units. These same elements appear time after time in different words, which are distinguished from one another by different arrangements of the elements—sometimes a very slight difference. If the words of our language were each as different from one another as a footstep is from a dog's bark, for example, perhaps Viki would learn them as easily as we do.

We have recently tested her ability to understand recombinations of familiar words within a sentence. For instance, she performs perfectly on "Kiss me" and "Bring me the dog." When we first said, "KISS the DOG," Viki did nothing at all. We coached her so that she might see what we were expecting her to do. Then we presented the second group: "Bring me a cup. Kiss me. KISS the CUP." This took fewer coachings, which indicated that some learning had taken place. Subsequent series took increasingly less time until "Kiss me. Give me your hand. KISS your HAND" was almost instantly comprehended. We will do more of this work as more nouns and action verbs become available to her.

We anticipate that Viki will understand more and more of what we say as time goes on, but we doubt that her comprehension will ever go further than simple commands and the names of things. And without more involved language, with only gestural demonstrations, a teacher can transmit very little knowledge to his pupil. It is only when I consider how much we rely on the few words she does understand that I realize how much less we will be able to teach her than could be given to a human child her age.

One can become educated without talking. But listening and understanding opens to a man the wisdom of the ages. It adds to his meager personal talents and experience the accumulated thought of countless men before him. Where does that leave one small ape who can't quite remember which are her ears and which are her eyes?

CHAPTER 28.

The Nature of the Beast

WE ARE often asked, "Since you have been educating this chimpanzee for three years, and since she has never lived with her own kind, just how much of a chimpanzee *is* she at this point?"

It is probable that Viki has become more indoctrinated with our culture than any three-year-old ape in history. However, in matters untouched by education, she remains completely chimpanzee. Physically, she is prettier and healthier than most of her kind, but she has the same black hair, eyebrow ridges, big ears, and preference for walking on all fours. Her face slopes down and out to a wide mouth. This facial structure accounts for her habit—often mistaken for nearsightedness—of bringing objects under scrutiny very close to her face. In this way she can see, taste, and smell the article under consideration while examining it with her delicate, flexible lips. If need be, it is also handy to the teeth, which, in spite of all training, remain her best weapon.

The chimpanzee's hand differs from the human's in having an extremely short, rather weak thumb. Many students, mindful of the ape's lack of culture, lay the blame on this inferior thumb. Viki's hand does not manipulate as cleverly as a child's, nor can she aspire to the concert piano or the art of engraving on pinheads. However, on a purely practical level, Viki is able to handle most of the tools of our culture as adequately as a child her age.

On a recent occasion a gentleman stood beside our car, telling me that Viki's short thumb was the whole answer to man's superiority. As he discoursed, Viki turned the ignition off and on, worked the windshield wiper, shifted gears, and rolled down the window, the better to swat the gentleman's little boy.

One aspect of our experiment has been to observe in Viki the unfolding of various *innately determined* behavior patterns, which have come to be regarded as typical of her species. These activities would arise free of any prompting on our part and without Viki's observation of the Laboratory apes, from whom she has been isolated with little more than a passing glance. We have been fortunate in seeing at close hand the development of many such modes of behavior. However, for all our study, we have been unsuccessful in finding a single normal chimpanzee activity which is not also engaged in to some extent by human beings.

The random play of a young ape left to its own devices is a rough-and-tumble whirl of running, jumping, and climbing. Viki endlessly gallops about her house and yard, and with an easy grace scurries up the woodwork and the trees. Yet such boundless energy cannot be attributed to the nature of the chimpanzee, but rather to the nature of young mammals in general. Any chimp would have felt at home among the companions of my own youth, for we supplemented our constant locomotion with bicycles, jumping ropes, scooters, roller skates, and pogo sticks. We saw no point in walking the earth if there was a fence to teeter along. Having exhausted the few

neighborhood trees, we aged our parents with flying leaps from
windows, down staircases, and off the roofs of houses.

One of the few things which can distract Viki from her perpetual motion is for any strange animal to wander into the
Pecan Grove. She immediately ceases all play to chase away
the intruder—provided it is taken in by her bluffing chimp
offensive. If it holds its ground, Viki retreats to mama's skirts.

At the Laboratory, the chimpanzee youngsters may be seen
practicing this bluff on each other. Like cute little miniatures of
King Kong they stand upright, shoulders hunched forward
and arms held out to the sides as they descend upon the enemy.
Then comes the crucial moment as the contestants face each
other, a tense moment of scowling, hand-clapping, foot-pound-
ing. The one most easily bluffed eventually yields to the other's
terrifying countenance and retreats in a windmilling scramble
of arms and legs.

Analogous behavior can be seen among the children of any
human community. My childhood friends were constantly preoccupied with establishing a dominance hierarchy. An out-
standing variation from the apes was our liberal use of the
human gift of speech. At the moment when we tried to out-
stare and outbluff our enemy, for example, we engaged in such
challenging repartee as, "Oh yeah?" "Yeah!" "Yeah?" "Yeah!"
"Sez you!" "Sez me!" Considering the never-ending aggression,
there was very little actual fighting.

The peculiar anthropoid behavior called "rocking" is said
to be an expression of anxiety. It consists of swaying the body
from side to side in a slow rhythm. Undoubtedly, worry causes
apes to rock, but close observation of Viki has shown that
rocking arises from a number of situations other than fear-
provoking ones.

Viki began rocking in her crib at six weeks of age with no apparent cause for alarm. During her infancy, immediately upon waking, she would lean on her elbows and rock, rock, rock, until I picked her up. At her scary phase, from three to five months of age, she rocked whenever worried, which was most of the time. Today she is infinitely less skittish than her baby kinfolk at the Laboratory, so that she seldom rocks in anxiety. However, when sleepy, bored, or restless, she will occasionally rock from side to side.

To a woman visitor who commented upon it, I described the Laboratory babies rocking in their cages like so many clock pendulums in a clock shop window. I was about to add that we had also seen this "chimpy" reaction in institutions for sick, deserted, or feeble-minded children, when she blurted out that her son had rocked this very way as a baby whenever he was nervous, sleepy, or bored. I said no more for I know that her son made Phi Beta Kappa at college, had a distinguished military career, and is now a successful businessman. Since then many mothers have told me that their children rocked as babies, and some of them have defensively pointed out certain adult variations of rocking which are acceptable in our society: thumb-twirling, leg-swinging, pencil-drumming, and pacing the floor, to mention a few.

The point of the following story is not to show how early my circle of friends included some on the anthropoid level, but as preface to the most "chimpy" behavior I can describe: In the home of a girlhood friend, I sometimes witnessed a strange ritual. The mother would glance up from her sewing and stare intently at the father. Then she would say, "That shirt you have on is a disgrace, absolutely beyond mending. I guess it's done for."

That was the cue. Instantly the two children would pounce

upon their father, or more specifically, upon the doomed shirt. Into each small hole they would insert their fingers and, with great shouts of joy, rip the shirt to shreds. While he pretended a huge struggle, they tugged and tore until all that remained was the collar around his neck and the button panel hanging down his front. Then they all collapsed in laughter at the sight of him. Thus allowed periodic vent to a primitive urge, they restrained themselves admirably in the time between wornout shirts. I had never seen the like of those shirt-tearings until I made the acquaintance of Viki and her grooming instinct.

Zoo visitors often see an ape or a monkey scratch himself or a companion, seem to find something, stare at it closely, and pop it into his mouth. Theorists in the crowd may diagnose this as a case of fleas, or say that the animal is hunting for salty flecks of dandruff. Chances are that he is picking because he cannot help himself, for apes and monkeys are driven by a powerful instinct to groom.

With the older chimpanzees at the Laboratory, grooming assumes the nature of a social responsibility, so that from time to time, Viki's father, Bokar, for instance, will squat down beside a cagemate, and very earnestly begin turning back its hair, bit by bit, while he searches the skin. As his busy fingers flick off a bit of dirt here, a loose hair or a piece of dandruff there, his tongue and lips make smacking noises, and his eyes stare with a concentration not often seen in a chimpanzee. Later he will be groomed by the friend, for this behavior has the social give and take of a favor received for every service rendered.

We were able to observe in Viki a complete development of the chimpanzee grooming instinct. The first signs appeared when she was eight weeks old, during her exercise periods on our bed. The calico comforter which I used as a bedspread was flecked at intervals with wool ties, and these fascinated Viki.

Lying on her stomach, she picked at them with her finger. Then one day she began picking at the small floral print of the calico. She put her mouth to a little yellow flower in the pattern, and moved her lips like a goldfish at feeding time.

Her mouth and fingers did not move together at grooming until she was six months old. By then this behavior had already become her most serious occupation. She looked possessed, with her eyes protruding, her tongue flashing in and out, and her forefingers scratching away at our hair, our glasses, a hole in our clothes, or whatever else had seized her attention. Her system was to pick a while, then mouth the offensive spot, perhaps adding a bit of saliva, and then scratch some more.

Between one year and eighteen months, several noises began to accompany her grooming fingers. One was the Bronx cheer. Another was a kissing sound, or more accurately, a sucking-in of air through smacking lips. The most shocking noise, combined with her intense grooming expression, was a rapid clacking together of her molars.

At eighteen months, in addition to grooming glaring defects, she began *searching* our hands for places to groom, in the systematic spirit of a chore. At two years she engaged in her first *self*-grooming of scratches, freckles, spots of dirt. Not until almost three years of age did she *look* for groom-worthy places on her own person. At first, this consisted of merely tugging at the hair on her thighs and belly, and staring at the chalky skin underneath. Now she gives herself several daily goings-over, squeezing out removable imperfections with the fingernails of her index fingers.

When she grooms us Viki is very persistent. If we put our hand over a hole which she has discovered, she tugs at the hand, screams furiously, and flops down and rocks, meanwhile glaring at us in a way that fully expresses her outrage at this violation of chimpanzee etiquette. In her turn, Viki is never so quiet as when we groom her. We find this a handy tool at the end of a strenuous day. She goes into a virtual trance as Keith turns back her hair, inch by inch, scratching now and then, and clacking his tongue. She sometimes places his hand on a spot which she apparently feels needs grooming. If he resists, she pushes the finger to get it started.

Here, then, is an instinct, predetermined and inevitable. It developed in Viki as she matured, as in all the chimps before her. It was free of education, for she had never seen a chimpanzee grooming. "Here," we told ourselves, "is one behavior pattern which is pure chimpanzee. People do not groom."

Of course, there were those shirt-tearings. And during the war Keith had to restrain me constantly from picking at the numerous stickers which we were required to paste on our windshield. There are some mothers who search their children's hair incessantly, some people who can't leave a scab alone, and a whole world of head scratchers, blackhead pickers, and thread removers, but none of these humans display the dedication of a chimpanzee grooming. There is no comparison with Viki's compelling movements of tongue and fingers, the terrifying noises, and the intense expression on her face.

I was recently trying to keep her away from a hole in the T-shirt of a little boy visitor. Viki insisted, but I insisted louder. Finally the boy's mother urged me to let Viki pick at the hole if she wanted to. "That shirt is about done for," was the phrase she used, and added to the boy, "We know all about this, don't we, dear?"

"You see," she explained to me, "when my son was a baby, I often let him exercise on my bed. Well, if there was the tiniest hole in a sheet, I might as well give it up for lost. He would find it every time, stick his finger into it, and rrrrrrrip! He just *had* to do it! And such an intense expression on his face! Honestly, Mrs. Hayes, it was terrifying."

CHAPTER 29.

It's Only the Beginning

THE question which visitors most frequently ask is: How long will you be able to keep her? Presumably they have seen full-grown chimpanzees in circus cages or at the zoo—short, stocky animals with long, powerful arms and many large teeth. These hundred-pound bundles of might and muscle could scarcely fit into the human way of life on an apartment-sized scale.

It is very difficult for me to visualize Viki grown into the size and form of her parents, but I know that in another ten years, this must inevitably come to pass. How long *will* Viki be acceptable in a human home? How long *will* we be able to keep her?

Since no man can predict the future, Viki, like the rest of us, must largely wait and see. Still we must make some plans, for when an animal is incapable of directing its own future, its guardians must strain their resources and their foresight to leave as little as possible to chance.

We do not think that Viki would be any happier in a cage than we would be, yet she obviously will never be able to

239

make her way independently in the world of humans. Therefore, we plan to keep Viki with us always, making whatever
arrangements are necessary. We have been altering our house
almost constantly since she arrived. Today she has a room of
her own; someday we will build a house with a special apartment for her, constructed of attractive but strong materials to
match her own strength. Today she has a fenced-in play yard;
someday the yard will be larger and the fence will be higher.
And so it goes, a continual adjustment in the interests of Viki's
happiness—which is essential to the success of our work.

The question often arises in the village drugstore as to
whether Viki will "turn on" us as she grows older. Among our
acquaintances are the Noells, who operate the traveling Gorilla
Show. We have seen their ten-year-old daughter playing with
an unmuzzled, unchained adult chimpanzee. When she tickled
it, the ape rolled on the floor and chuckled like an overgrown
Viki. I would also like to point out that both the late Gargantua
and his "mate" Toto were raised by human foster parents without assault. On the other hand, the newspapers carry many
an account of a berserk human who has murdered his gray-
haired mother or father or both. It's a chance parents have to
take.

In the immediate future we intend to redouble our efforts
to improve communication with Viki, investigating all possible
nonlanguage forms of conveying information—gestures, pictures and demonstration. We will also try to give her more
human speech, realizing that the amount is bound to be very
limited. We expect her to learn several more whispered words,
and at present she is perfecting the voiced word "up," with
which she asks for a piggyback ride.

The significance of Viki's speech training lies not in the

fact that she has learned a few words, but rather in her great difficulty in doing so, and in keeping them straight afterward. We are beginning to suspect that this tendency to confuse the words she knows may merely be the most obvious result of a more general inability to retain large numbers of arbitrary associations without conflict.

The average human has many thousands of these associations at his command, and is annoyed with himself when he occasionally "can't think of" a certain word.

Chimpanzees are often thought to lag behind the human in various "higher mental functions." We have found no such failing in Viki, thus far, and are inclined to offer the tentative suggestion that man's advantage may lie in his greater facility with the "lower mental functions" of learning and remembering. Such an advantage might not be apparent where a simple, isolated association is concerned; but where many of them must be handled at once, man may have a greater resistance to mutual confusion among them.

We plan to test this possibility by studying Viki's ability to learn and remember a large number of visual, nonlanguage associations. We will compare her performance with those of Laboratory chimps, normal human children, and deaf children. This last group is included, because they are like Viki in being unable to use language. If we should find that their performance, as well as Viki's, is inferior to that of hearing children, we would have to conclude that the ability to retain, unconfused, a large number of symbols, is not innate to a species, but rather a learned skill, and that it is dependent upon language.

Perhaps, as time goes on, we will be able to tell Viki many things with drawings which we cannot tell her by words. We are about to test Viki's comprehension of pictures, by having her select one object from an assortment to match the photograph we hold up.

Soon, also, we will show her a movie of us doing the items of the Imitation Series, to see if she can imitate the motion picture. If she succeeds, we will show her still photos of us clapping our hands, tugging at our ears, patting our head, and so on, asking her to "do this" from the picture alone.

We will continue comparing Viki with Laboratory apes. There are certain problems which usually stump caged apes completely, although the tasks look absurdly simple to people. We are anxious to see how Viki will perform on these.

For example, an ape is allowed to see a piece of fruit being hidden in one of two dissimilar containers; the containers are then removed from view for thirty seconds, after which they are presented to the ape in different positions. The animal seems unable to remember which one contains the fruit.

His failure may be due to lack of experience with containers, in which case we would expect Viki to do much better. However, the test typically involves many trials, in rapid succession. Therefore, perhaps the difficulty is due, once again, to confusion among a large number of associations. If this is the case, Viki will probably have no advantage.

Viki is at an age when the human child would be starting nursery school. Since it is impractical to send Viki off to school, she will be given the usual curriculum of the nursery school in her own home; at least such things as painting, cutting and pasting, clay modeling, and similar items where language is not essential.

Lyla Kleemeier has just started a nursery school in Orange Park, where I will have the privilege of studying her technique while observing the reactions of her human students. I came home from my first few visits to the school very impressed with the superiority of the human Threes over Viki, and by their great differences. But as I took up my day with Viki, I was again overwhelmed by the similarities. I mentioned this to Lyla, and she reported having received the same impression when she worked with language-retarded human children who were otherwise intelligent.

As Viki grows, the number of problems which might be profitably studied with her grows proportionately greater. Recently the number was making us a bit panicky. Where would we find time to do all our work with her, with normal children, with deaf children, with caged apes, in addition to writing reports, building apparatus, compiling our movies and photographic record, as well as keeping our house in repair? Then, to our relief, the Samuel S. Fels fund made us a grant to provide a graduate student assistant. In the coming year, our work will thus be divided among three people, instead of two.

We still look upon our experiment as being in its early stages. Viki is only three years old, and it cannot be assumed that she has completed a greater proportion of her intellectual development than a child has at her age. Viki may in some way partially sidestep her natural language failing to become a genius of her species. Or deficits other than language may appear later, and change all our present conclusions. We are very curious to see what lies ahead.

Author's Note—
Books You Might Enjoy

IN THE care and education of Viki, we have been greatly helped and stimulated by the experiences of others who had previously taken apes into their lives. Those readers who have laughed and struggled with us through Viki's first three years will perhaps enjoy reading the books which we found most valuable.

My Friends, the Apes, by Belle Benchley. 1942. Boston, Little, Brown.

As Director of the magnificent San Diego Zoo, Mrs. Benchley is in an excellent position to observe and report the life and psychology of the zoo apes.

Apes, by Winifred Felce. 1948. London, Chapman & Hall.

Here is the finest practical guide we have encountered to the requirements of caged apes. By an Englishwoman who was responsible for the well-being of a large colony of them, it has proved fascinating reading to many of our friends who have no practical need for it.

Toto and I, by Augusta Maria Hoyt. 1941. Philadelphia, New York, J. B. Lippincott.

Toto, the gorilla, eventually became known to the world as Gargantua's "mate." This is the touching story of her early life with Mrs. Hoyt, who raised her from infancy.

My Friend, Toto, by Cherry Kearton. 1925. London, Arrowsmith.

This Toto was a chimpanzee who accompanied Mr. Kearton on an African trip. Their adventures in the Congo, and their journey to London, make lively reading, and inspire great respect for the intelligence of Mr. Kearton's little friend.

The Ape and the Child, by W. N. Kellogg and L. A. Kellogg. 1933. New York, McGraw-Hill.

Twenty years ago, the Kelloggs adopted the seven-month-old chimpanzee, Gua, into their home, and compared her with their baby son. During her nine months in the human environment, Gua's behavior and accomplishments resemble Viki's, at that age, to a striking degree.

Animals Are My Hobby, by Gertrude Lintz. 1942. New York, McBride.

At her home in Brooklyn, Mrs. Lintz has raised a great many apes, many of whom later became show performers or circus attractions. One of these was the late Gargantua, whom we meet in this book as Buddy, a charming youngster, dependent upon people for love and protection, in no sense the ferocious beast of the circus posters.

The Great Apes, by Robert M. Yerkes and Ada Yerkes. 1929. New Haven, Yale University Press.

This scholarly book, by the founder of our Laboratory and his fellow scientist, Mrs. Yerkes, has been in constant reference in our house. It is *the* book of ape information.

Chimpanzees, by Robert M. Yerkes. 1943. New Haven, Yale University Press.

Here is the story of the Yerkes Laboratories of Primate Biology and its inhabitants. In the well-organized text and fine illustrations, the reader may see Viki's relatives living the laboratory way of life and taking part in many important experiments.